MOSBY'S RAIDS
IN
CIVIL WAR
NORTHERN VIRGINIA

WILLIAM S. CONNERY

SERIES EDITOR DOUGLAS W. BOSTICK

Charleston | London

THE
History
PRESS

Published by The History Press
Charleston, SC 29403
www.historypress.net

Copyright © 2013 by William S. Connery
All rights reserved

Front cover: Fire in the Valley, by John Paul Strain.
Back cover: Colonel John Singleton Mosby. Courtesy of the Library of Congress.

First published 2013

Manufactured in the United States

ISBN 978.1.60949.893.1

Library of Congress CIP data applied for.

Contents

Acknowledgements

I want to thank and recognize those who are currently keeping the spirit of Mosby alive in Northern Virginia. Tom Evans and Don Hakenson have given strong encouragement for this book. Tom is the preeminent Mosby scholar in the area. His book, *Mosby's Confederacy: A Guide to the Roads and Sites of Colonel John Singleton Mosby*, is still the best tour book for Mosby sites in Virginia. Don, my neighbor in Rose Hill (where Mosby captured Colonel Dulany), twice a year escorts a bus full of enthusiasts to discover for themselves the places where Mosby lived and raided. Don has also written several books on Mosby and the Franconia–Rose Hill section of Fairfax County. Together with Chuck Mauro and Steve Sherman, Don has written, produced and narrated the award-winning film *Mosby's Combat Operations in Fairfax County, Virginia*. Don is also director of the Stuart-Mosby Cavalry Museum, located in the historic section of Centreville, Virginia, where John Ward assisted me in photographing the museum's Mosby memorabilia.

I also want to acknowledge a few other people who are active in Mosby events throughout Northern Virginia. Rich Gillespie is current director of education of the Mosby Heritage Area Association (MHAA) in Middleburg, which presents Mosby-themed programs throughout the year. The headquarters of the MHAA is located in the house near where Mosby officially organized his Rangers in June 1863. Rich is also the narrator of a Mosby-themed episode of *Get Lost in Loudoun*. Dave Goetz, who recently published a book on the relationship between Mosby and U.S. Grant (*Hell Is Being a Republican in Virginia*), also conducts private tours through Mosby's

Civil War–era map of Mosby's Confederacy in Northern Virginia, including parts of Maryland and West Virginia. *Author's collection.*

Confederacy. Eric Buckland has written several books, focusing on the men who rode with Mosby. The Mosby Players, led by Paula Johnson, portray Mosby; his wife, Pauline; and other characters from the Civil War. The group also gives tours of Mosby's adopted hometown of Warrenton, the city where he practiced law after the war and where he and his wife are buried. There are at least two gentlemen—Jimmy Fleming and Gary Carroll—who portray Colonel Mosby at educational events throughout the region.

Introduction

John Singleton Mosby, the "Gray Ghost" of Northern Virginia, remains one of the most fascinating and controversial partisan raiders to serve the Confederacy during the Civil War. With absolutely no military training, he rose from private to colonel based on the effectiveness of his tactics, especially in the latter half of the war. His most daring raids—capturing a Union general in March 1863 and a Union colonel in September 1863—occurred in Fairfax County, well behind Yankee lines. He was the Rebel officer most mentioned in dispatches by General Robert E. Lee, whose only complaint was that Mosby tended to be wounded too often. It is believed he prolonged the war by at least six months by harassing the Manassas Gap Railroad in 1864 and kept from combat anywhere from ten thousand to forty thousand Union troops. His raiders came not only from Northern Virginia but also from other sections of the Old Dominion, together with volunteers from Maryland, England, Scotland, Ireland and Germany—and even Union deserters!

Before the war, Mosby was a staunch Unionist. But when his native state of Virginia decided to leave the Union, he followed its lead, volunteering his services as a private. His daringness and resourcefulness brought him to the attention of J.E.B. Stuart, the Confederate cavalry leader. After one and a half years in Stuart's service (it was Mosby's scouting that convinced Stuart of the feasibility of his ride around Union general George B. McClellan in June 1862), Mosby was given permission to conduct independent guerrilla operations in Northern Virginia in January 1863. He officially called his

Rangers into service at Rector's Cross Roads near Middleburg in June 1863. Until April 1865, Mosby led hit-and-run commando raids throughout Northern Virginia, often venturing into West Virginia, Maryland and even Pennsylvania during the Gettysburg Campaign.

Normally, cavalry on the march sent up a humming sound that could be heard for hundreds of yards at night. Sabers and scabbards clanked, canteens jingled and hooves clattered. Mosby, carefully practicing stealth, forbade sabers, canteens and clanking equipment; his column moved so quietly that civilians lying in their beds in houses next to the road recognized when Mosby's men were passing only by the sound of their hoofbeats. Near the target, he would veer off into soft fields or woods, and it was so quiet that the men could hear whippoorwills calling in the distance.

"Silence! Pass it back," he ordered, and from that point, he directed only with hand signals. If attacking dismounted, he would have the men remove their spurs and leave them with the horse-holders. He walked in soft snow or used the sound of the rain and wind to cover footsteps and once timed his final pounce with the sound of coughing by a Union horse. "We made no noise," he wrote, and one of his men recalled, "Our men were in among the prostrate forms of the Yankees before they were fairly awake, and they assisted some of them to unwind from their blankets."

Modern military studies of sleep deprivation indicate that cognitive skills deteriorate after one night without sleep; after two or three nights, performance is considerably impaired. Confederate general John Hunt Morgan's men were falling asleep on the road during his Indiana–Ohio Raid of June–July 1863, and his exhausted scouts failed him at Buffington Island by reporting that the ford was guarded by regular forces when they were only a few frightened home guards. General Abel D. Streight became groggy from exhaustion and sleep deprivation on a raid in Alabama in the spring of 1863, and Confederate general Nathan Bedford Forrest deceived him into surrendering to a force less than half his size. Union general H. Judson Kilpatrick became worn down and lost his nerve in his raid on Richmond, Virginia, with Colonel Ulric Dahlgren early in 1864 and was driven away by defenders that he outnumbered six to one. But Mosby carefully saved the energy of his men and horses, moving slowly into a raid for maximum performance in the fight and hasty withdrawal. He preferred to strike at about 4:00 a.m., when guards were least alert and reserves most soundly asleep. He said that it was easy to surround sleeping men and that it took five minutes for a man to awaken out of a deep sleep and fully react.

Mosby and his men wore Confederate uniforms on missions so that they could claim their rights as prisoners of war if captured. They were always accused of masquerading as the enemy. During cold weather, they wore dark overcoats, and when they had Union prisoners, they would place them in front to create the appearance of Union cavalry. They usually marched in a leisurely style, like friends out for a ride, but for disguise they would form column of fours and appear to be well-drilled blueclads.

When it rained, they wore dark rubber ponchos, which were standard issue for both North and South, convenient for approaching the enemy with revolvers drawn, concealed under the rain garments.

Mosby achieved the objective of using fear as a force multiplier, diverting many times his own number from the Union army and creating disruptions and false alarms. He seemed to possess a sixth sense enabling him to anticipate enemy weaknesses. Like an entrepreneur forecasting the business cycle, he had a tremendous instinct to select targets at the opportune time and place for maximum impact. Part of it was vigilance and alert scouting, but Mosby's record of locating and attacking weaknesses in enemy defenses was almost uncanny. A Union cavalry officer in the Army of the Potomac recognized it when he wrote, "Even now, from the tops of the neighboring mountains, his hungry followers are looking down upon our weak points."

Time and again, Mosby danced on the nerves of opponents where they were most vulnerable. Union general Philip Sheridan had great personal pride in his ability as a cavalry and supply officer, and one of the last things he wanted was to have some of his wagons captured by guerrillas. General Henry W. Halleck feared that Mosby would make headlines on his watch defending Washington City and stain his reputation. Elizabeth Custer worried that Mosby might capture her beloved new husband, George Armstrong. Mosby's psychological war even went to the extent of sending a lock of his hair to President Abraham Lincoln; even though it was only a joke, it reminded Lincoln that outside the Washington City defense perimeter, Mosby reigned.

Mosby realized that making his name feared would give his warfare greater emotional impact. He insisted that his men make it clear when they attacked that they were "Mosby's Men." Rangers learned that the word *Mosby* was so powerful that it was useful in subduing a guard and preventing him from yelling or shooting. "I am Mosby," a Ranger would whisper, and sometimes the captive would go into a daze, bowing his head and trembling in fear. When ordered to walk, prisoners staggered as if drunk, some became nauseated and vomited and others fell on their knees and raised their hands, pleading for their lives. When a Union soldier disappeared, his friends would say, "Mosby had gobbled him up."

Union opponents said Mosby's men seemed to be almost intangible demons and devils, and myth claimed that when they scattered into the mountains, the tracks of their horses suddenly disappeared. "Nobody ever saw one," a Union officer wrote. "They leave no tracks, and they come down upon you when you least expect them." Northern journalists characterized them as "rebel devils," "horse thieves," "skulking guerillas," "a gang of murderers and highway robbers," "cut-throats," "picket-shooting assassins," "marauding highwaymen" and "lawless banditti." Union horsemen named their area "a nest of guerrillas," "Devil's Corner," "The Trap" and "Mosby's Confederacy."

By the close of the war, he had made himself the single most-hated Confederate in the North. Northern newspapers designated him "the devil," "Robin Hood," "horse thief," "bushwhacker," "marauding highwayman," "murderer," "notorious land pirate" and "guerrilla chief." His main title as the Gray Ghost survives to this day. *Jack Mosby, the Guerrilla*, a dime novel published in 1867, described him as a tall and powerful desperado with a black beard; a cruel, remorseless man who enjoyed cutting men apart with his tremendous saber and riddling them with bullets from pistols on his belt. In the book, he had his sweetheart lure Union officers into his hands and delighted in hanging them by their arms and kindling a fire under their feet to force them to talk. In the cheap woodcut on the cover, he appeared in a room in the Astor House in New York City, pouring Greek fire on his bed. This was based on an actual incidence of Confederate agents using incendiary devices in New York City in November 1864. Mosby was so hated that into the next generation he remained the boogeyman; Northern mothers quieted their children by saying, "Hush, child, Mosby will get you!"

On the other side, Southerners admired Mosby as a great hero. His portrait appeared in the book *The War and Its Heroes*, published in Richmond in 1864. Southern journalists considered him a "daring and distinguished guerilla chief" who made the country seem literally alive with guerrillas. Southern people named babies for him and told the tale that one day in the Shenandoah Valley a Union officer knocked on the door of a plantation house. A female slave answered the door, and he asked if anybody was home. "Nobody but Mosby," she answered. "Is *Mosby* here?" he inquired excitedly. "Yes," she answered, and he jumped on his horse and rode away. Shortly, he returned, surrounding the house with a company of cavalry. He

Colonel Mosby and his men. *Author's collection.*

came to the door and asked if Mosby was still there. "Yes," the woman said, inviting him in. "Where is he?" he demanded, and she pointed to her infant son in a cradle and proudly announced, "There he is. I call him 'Mosby,' sir. 'Colonel Mosby,' that's his name!"

Probably the highest praise that Mosby received in the war appeared in the *Richmond Whig* on October 18, 1864. He had been in Richmond a short time before, convalescing from a wound, and a few days later had returned to duty and raided Salem, temporarily halting Union construction on the Manassas Gap Railroad, and he had struck the B&O Railroad with the Greenback Raid:

> *The indomitable and irrepressible Mosby is again in the saddle carrying destruction and consternation in his path. One day in Richmond wounded and eliciting the sympathy of every one capable of appreciating the daring deeds of the boldest and most successful partisan leader the war has produced—three days afterwards surprising and scattering a Yankee force at Salem as if they were frightened sheep fleeing before a hungry wolf—and then before the great mass of the people are made aware of the particulars of this dashing achievement, he has swooped around and cut the Baltimore and Ohio railroad—the great artery of communication between East and*

Medal given to John Singleton Mosby as one of the first inductees into the U.S. Army Rangers' Hall of Fame in 1992. *Courtesy of the Stuart-Mosby Cavalry Museum.*

West, capturing a mail train and contents, and constituting himself, by virtue of the strength of his own right arm, and the keen blade it wields, a receiver of army funds for the United States. If he goes on as he has commenced since the slight bleeding the Yankees gave him, who can say that in time we will not be able to pay our army off in greenbacks. If he has not yet won a Brigadier's wreath upon his collar, the people have placed upon his brow one far more enduring.

In April 1865, almost two weeks after General Lee's surrender at Appomattox Court House, Mosby tried to work out a deal with General Winfield Scott Hancock, who had replaced General Sheridan in the Shenandoah Valley. The negotiations fell through, and Mosby simply disbanded his Rangers, never actually surrendering. After the war, seeking to bring about reconciliation of the North and South, he aligned himself with the Republican Party—even campaigning for President Ulysses S. Grant in 1872! (Mosby said at that time, "The closest thing to Hell is being a Republican in Virginia.") He attempted to set up a law practice in his adopted hometown of Warrenton, county seat of Fauquier, until someone took a shot at him at the train station, and following the advice of President Rutherford B. Hayes, he was appointed U.S. Consul to Hong Kong.

Moving back to the United States in the mid-1880s, Mosby became a lawyer for the Southern Pacific Railroad in San Francisco. It was there that he met a young man whose grandfather and great-uncles had fought as officers for the Confederacy. Mosby rode out with him, acting as himself and having the young man pretend to be Robert E. Lee. The boy later went to Virginia Military Institute, then West Point, and he used the tactics he learned from the Gray Ghost as a tank commander in World War II. His name was General George S. Patton Jr. The U.S. Army Ranger Association recognizes Mosby and his Rangers as part of their history.

CHAPTER 1

The Early Years

1833–1860

John Singleton Mosby was born December 6, 1833, at Edgemont in Powhatan County, Virginia, to Virginia McLaurine Mosby and Alfred Daniel Mosby, a graduate of Hampden-Sydney College. His father was a member of an old Virginia family of English origin whose ancestor, Richard Mosby, was born in England in 1600 and settled in Charles City County in the early seventeenth century. Mosby's mother claimed descent from the Scottish Patriot Rob Roy MacGregor, made famous in Sir Walter Scott's novel *Rob Roy*. Mosby was named after his paternal grandfather, John Singleton. So Mosby can be considered a member of the First Families of Virginia (FFVs).

Mosby began his education at a school called Murrell's Shop. When he started school, his mother insisted that he be accompanied by the house slave, Aaron Burton. After the two-mile walk, Burton was supposed to return home. Mosby convinced him to wait outside at least until noon. When the break came, Mosby was one of the last students out and was horrified to find some of the older boys "auctioning off" Burton. Mosby pounced on the auctioneer, while Burton ran off to home. The boys tried to convince him that they were just joking. Thus began Mosby's predilection to fight for what he believed was right.

Mosby was also interested and engrossed in reading. When the other children went outside for recess or lunch, he would often stay, reading his favorite books. The story that greatly influenced him was that of Francis Marion, the South Carolinian "Swamp Fox" of Revolutionary War fame. Colonel Marion showed himself to be a singularly able leader of irregular

The site of Mosby's boyhood home in Powhatan County, Central Virginia. *Author's collection.*

militiamen. Unlike the Continental troops, Marion's Men, as they were known, served without pay and supplied their own horses, arms and often their own food.

Marion rarely committed his men to frontal warfare, but he repeatedly surprised larger bodies of Loyalists or British regulars with quick surprise attacks and equally sudden withdrawal from the field. Mosby applied these lessons twenty years later as he fought against a foreign invader. Mel Gibson's character, Benjamin Martin, in the 2000 movie *The Patriot* is partly based on Colonel Marion. In this movie, Martin is often referred to by the British as a ghost. Moby's most popular title is the Gray Ghost.

After two months, Mosby was sent to the Widow Frye's school. Murrell's Shop closed because the teacher one day went home for lunch, got drunk and was found in a ditch by the side of the road. The older boys got him back to school. It was his example that led Mosby to abstain from hard liquor for the rest of his life.

His family moved farther west to Albemarle County, near Charlottesville, where the education opportunities were more abundant, with eighteen academies. Because of his small stature and frail health, Mosby was the victim of bullies throughout his school career. The eldest survivor of eleven children (one older sister had died in infancy), Mosby could stay home and read and not be responsible for farm duties. Instead of becoming withdrawn and lacking in self-confidence, the boy responded by fighting back, although Mosby later in his life stated that he never won any fight in which he was engaged. In fact, the only time he did not lose a fight was when an adult stepped in and broke it up.

While Mosby went to a local academy, his sisters were tutored at home by a governess, Miss Abby Southwick from Massachusetts. She was an ardent abolitionist. She was friendly toward Mosby and spoke about the evils of slavery. But he wondered why it was so bad to be a slave. He was very fond of the slaves his father owned, and they seemed to be happy and well cared for.

On October 3, 1850, he entered the University of Virginia, taking classical studies and joining the Washington Literary Society and Debating Union. He excelled in Latin, Greek and literature (all of which he enjoyed), but mathematics was a problem for him. In his third year, a quarrel erupted between Mosby and a notorious bully, George R. Turpin, a tavern keeper's son who was stouter and stronger than Mosby. When Mosby heard from a friend that Turpin had insulted him, Mosby sent him a letter asking for an explanation—one of the rituals in the code of honor to which Southern gentlemen adhered. Turpin became enraged and declared that on their next meeting, he would "eat him up raw!" Mosby decided he had to meet Turpin despite the risk; to run away would be dishonorable.

On March 29, 1853, the two met, Mosby having brought with him a small pepper-box pistol in the hope of dissuading Turpin from an attack. When they met, Mosby said, "I hear you have been making assertions." Turpin put his head down and charged. At that point, Mosby pulled out the pistol and shot his adversary in the neck. The distraught nineteen-year-old Mosby went home to await his fate. He was arrested and arraigned on two charges: unlawful shooting (a misdemeanor with a maximum sentence of one year in jail and a $500 fine) and malicious shooting (a felony with a maximum sentence of ten years in the penitentiary). After a trial that almost resulted in a hung jury, Mosby was convicted of the lesser offense but received the maximum sentence. Mosby later discovered that he had been expelled from the university before he was brought to trial. There is nothing to suggest that Turpin, for all of his former violence, was likewise expelled for his notorious past.

While serving time in prison, Mosby won the friendship of his prosecutor, attorney William J. Robertson. When Mosby expressed his desire to study

First known image of Mosby, as a student at the University of Virginia in 1852. *Courtesy of the Stuart-Mosby Cavalry Museum.*

law, Robertson offered the use of his law library. Mosby studied law for the rest of his incarceration. Friends and family used political influence in an attempt to obtain a pardon. Governor Joseph Johnson reviewed the evidence and pardoned Mosby on December 23, 1853. In early 1854, his fine was rescinded by the state legislature. The incident, trial and imprisonment so traumatized Mosby that he never wrote about it in his memoirs.

Aristides Monteiro, a classmate who would later serve as a surgeon in Mosby's Rangers, said of him, "Of all my University friends and acquaintances this youthful prisoner would have been the last one I would have selected with the least expectation that the world would ever hear from him again."

After studying for months in Robertson's law office, Mosby was admitted to the bar and established his own practice in nearby Howardsville. About this time, Mosby met Pauline Clarke, who was visiting from out of town. He was Methodist and she was Catholic, but their courtship ensued. Her father, Beverly Leonidas Clarke, originally from Kentucky, was an active attorney, former member of Congress (serving from Tennessee in 1847–49, the same single term as another Kentuckian, Abraham Lincoln, who was representing Illinois at that time) and well-connected politician. They were married in a Nashville hotel on December 30, 1857. Among their wedding gifts was Aaron Burton, who gladly followed the master of his youth into his new home. After living for a year with Mosby's parents, the couple settled in Bristol, Virginia, right on the border of Tennessee and close to Pauline's hometown. They had two children before the Civil War, and another was born during it. They would eventually have eight children: four girls and four boys.

The presidential election of 1860 pitted four candidates against each other. The Republican Party submitted its second candidate, Abraham Lincoln (John C. Fremont had lost to Democrat James Buchanan in 1856). The Democrat Party split between Northern (Senator Stephen Douglas) and Southern (Vice President John C. Breckinridge) candidates. A fourth party, Constitutional Union, built on the ruins of the Know-Nothings, put forth John Bell. In Bristol and the surrounding area, most people supported Breckinridge and Bell. Mosby supported Douglas and on November 6 voted for him by voice, so all his neighbors knew where he stood. Actually, there was no secret ballot at that time. He spoke out against secession, and when an editorial was printed in the *Bristol News* in January 1861 in support of secession after several Deep South slave states had left the Union, Mosby predicted that secession would mean a long, bloody war, followed by a century of border feuding, and hinted that he would like to be the hangman for any secessionist.

All of this changed on April 12, when Fort Sumter was attacked, and again on April 15, when President Lincoln called for seventy-five thousand volunteers to invade the South. A Virginia Secession Convention had already been meeting for several months in Richmond and had voted twice to remain in the Union. But on April 17, the convention voted for secession, and Mosby, like his later commander, Robert E. Lee, cast his fate with his native state. In December 1860, Mosby had joined a local militia group, the Washington Mounted Rifles, who rarely met. But now their commander, Captain William "Grumble" Jones, called the company to arms, issued Confederate uniforms and told his men to put their home affairs in order. Mosby had joined the Confederate army as a private.

CHAPTER 2

Mosby Goes Off to War

1861

After a few weeks of drilling, Captain Jones got his men on the road to Richmond. The three-hundred-mile journey took eighteen days. At this point, Mosby weighed less than 125 pounds, slouched in his saddle and appeared to be the most unsoldierly one in his unit. Yet as the days rode past, his lungs cleared up, he could breathe freely, he enjoyed eating and he began to gain weight. Describing to his mother his experience of sleeping on the ground, he wrote, "I never before had such luxurious sleeping." After a few days in Richmond, the command moved several miles north to Ashland. His parents visited him there, bringing a box of food and his slave, Burton, to serve as his body servant. Burton would cook and take care of his horse and bodily needs for the remainder of the war.

In an interview he gave at the age of eighty-six when he was living in Brooklyn, New York, Aaron Burton was generous in his recollection of Mosby: "I raised Colonel Mosby. I loved him and was with him in all his battles. When the war was over Colonel John told me that I was free and could go and do as I pleased. He is a good man, and was a great fighter."

After the war, Mosby never denied that slavery was wrong or that it was the root cause of the war, but at the same time, it was important that he at least be regarded as a generous master.

While in camp, Mosby made only two real friends. One was Fountain Beattie, who became one of his Rangers and whom he remained close to his entire life. The other was his commander, Captain Jones. "Grumble" Jones had attended West Point (class of 1848) and served several years with the

Mosby's servant Aaron Burton later in life. He attended to Mosby throughout the war. Mosby freed him when the war ended. *Author's collection.*

U.S. Mounted Rifles on the frontier. He came home to Virginia on furlough to marry his sweetheart, Eliza Dunn, on January 13, 1852. Less than three months later, on a voyage to a new assignment in Texas, a storm came up that swept Eliza out of his arms and overboard, where she drowned. He blamed himself for her death, wishing that he could have saved her or drowned with her. He never remarried.

Jones was gruff with his men and insisted that they follow the fundamentals of military training. Mosby had picked a good mentor for his introduction into military life. Jones taught him the importance of vigilance, showed him how to enforce discipline fairly and, by example, demonstrated that the men appreciated efficient administration. Mosby valued Jones's teaching so highly that, when a friend offered to obtain Mosby an officer's commission, he declined, preferring to train as a private under Jones. If Robertson had made Mosby a lawyer, "Grumble" Jones was setting him on the path to becoming the Gray Ghost.

On July 1, as Jones's command was arriving at Bunker Hill in the Shenandoah Valley, Mosby saw for the first time his future commander, Lieutenant Colonel James Ewell Brown (Jeb) Stuart. Just ten months older than Mosby, Stuart weighed 180 pounds, with auburn hair and a full reddish beard. He was another West Pointer (class of 1854), had almost been killed by Cheyenne Indians and assisted Robert E. Lee in the capture of John Brown in October 1859. For Mosby, an aura of Victorian romance surrounded Stuart; he was a romantic cavalier, a brave fighter so gentle that on the western prairie, Stuart collected tiny flowers and feathers of small birds and pressed them into scrapbooks of clippings of cheerful, optimistic poems. Stuart was so unique that Mosby later wrote, "He seemed to defy all natural laws. I did not approach him, and little thought that I would ever rise from the ranks to intimacy with him."

After just ten days of scouting, Jones's troops took part in the screening of the Confederate army, allowing General Joe Johnston's withdrawal from the Valley to reinforce General Pierre G.T. Beauregard's army, ensconced on the banks of Bull Run in Northern Virginia. Jones's men remained mainly in reserve, until Union forces ran back in defeat toward Alexandria and Washington City, after the Battle of First Manassas/Bull Run on July 21. Mosby and his companions pursued the fleeing Yankees for six to eight miles, retrieving overcoats, tents, muskets and other items, along with capturing prisoners until dark. He expected the war to be over by the end of the year. Yet in analyzing First Manassas after the war, he argued that the Confederate cause was lost there because its advantage had not been exploited. He thought that if the available cavalry units, including Stuart's, had been ordered across the Potomac River above Washington City at Seneca Mills in Maryland, they could have moved toward Baltimore, cut communications and isolated Washington and possibly ended the war.

For the next six to eight months, Jones's Mounted Rifles spent most of their time on patrol and picket duty, often in sight of the enemy capital, Washington City. Just a week after the battle at Manassas, Mosby wrote to Pauline from Fairfax Court House:

> We have made no further advance and I know no more of contemplated movements than you do...A few nights ago we went down near Alexandria to stand as a picket (advance) guard. It was after dark. When riding along the road a volley was suddenly poured into us from a thick clump of pines. The balls whistled around us and Captain Jones' horse fell, shot through the head. We were perfectly helpless, as it was dark and they were concealed in the bushes. The best of it was that the Yankees shot three of their own men—thought they were ours...Beauregard has no idea of attacking Alexandria. When he attacks Washington he will go about Alexandria to attack Washington. No other news. For one week before the battle we had

an awful time—had about two meals during the whole time—marched two days and one night on one meal, in the rain, in order to arrive in time for the fight…We captured a great quantity of baggage left here by the Yankees; with orders for it to be forwarded to Richmond.

Generally during the war, both sides deployed cavalry as pickets or guards to serve as a tripwire defense to warn of an approaching enemy force. A line of companies spread across the front, with each company headquarters designated as the reserve and outposts or picket posts of four to six mounted men thrown forward one-half mile. The only one who stayed alert and mounted was the vidette, a man from the outpost positioned one hundred yards toward the enemy. Mosby enjoyed duty as a vidette, much preferring it to camp life, which he considered irksome. At a crossroads in Fairfax County, he would sit alone on his horse from midnight to daybreak, listening to the night sounds of the forest. He ate breakfast with the local people and, on scouts with the company, learned how to set an ambush among the dense pines and, when ambushed, remain calm and aim low.

It was during this time that Mosby had his first real brush with death. He wrote to his wife at the beginning of September:

I received your letter about two days ago and would have immediately replied but was unable to do so until now. I received a fall from my horse one day last week near Falls Church which came very near killing me. I have now entirely recovered and will return to camp this morning which is now about four miles from here [He was convalescing at Fairfax Court House]. *I was out on picket one dark and rainy night. There were only three of us at one post. A large body of cavalry came dashing down towards us from the direction of the enemy. Our orders were to fire on all. I fired my gun, started back towards where our main body was. My horse slipped down, fell on me and galloped off leaving me in a senseless condition in the road.*

Fortunately the body of cavalry turned out to be a company of our own men who had gone out after night to arrest a spy. When they started they promised Captain Jones to go by our post and inform us of the fact in order to prevent confusion. This they failed to do and their own culpable neglect of duty came near getting some of them killed.

I had no bones broken. I have been staying at the hospital here to recover. Captain Jones permitted my good friend Beattie to leave the company and come stay with me. He is still with me. Captain Jones will send my horse in for me in the morning. I was very kindly treated.

William "Grumble" Jones, Mosby's
first commander in the war.
Author's collection.

When Mosby was fully recovered, he was on picket duty one night within four miles of Washington City when he struck up a conversation with his Yankee counterparts. He invited them to supper, and under flag of truce, they accepted and ate with him. Off duty, he rode to Munson's Hill, about six miles from Washington City, to enjoy the view of the city, with its fortifications under construction and the Old Flag floating over the unfinished capitol building. For sport, he would ride out with the hay wagon and shoot Union guards on the opposite hill, then adjust the sights on his Sharps carbine by checking with a local woman on the effects of his bullets. "One of them was killed dead—shot through the head," he wrote Pauline. Describing shooting men in a cornfield, he declared, "I took a deliberate aim & fired at them with more eagerness than I ever did at a squirrel."

Although Mosby frequently saw Jeb Stuart, who now had his headquarters at Fairfax Court House, he had not met him personally until September 11, when Stuart took out three hundred men to scout the enemy. Near Lewinsville he picked out three men at random, one of them Mosby, and rode forward to reconnoiter. Out of the woods, within shooting distance, a force appeared. Mosby dismounted and took careful aim with his carbine at a smartly dressed officer. But Stuart stopped him, saying, "They might be our men." It was in Fairfax County that Stuart received his promotion to brigadier general on September 24.

On a scout near Falls Church with about eighty men, Mosby and Beattie became separated from the rest and suddenly came upon two Union soldiers. Mosby demanded their surrender, but they commenced firing. Mosby and Beattie each selected an opponent, and both sides exchanged several shots without effect. Mosby related, "I then jumped down from my horse, and as the fellow turned to run I rested my carbine against a tree & shot him dead. He never knew what struck him…After the fight was over I went & looked at the man I killed. The bullet had passed entirely through his head."

Confederate officers relied on Northern newspapers for news, and Mosby competed with other scouts to be first to bring a paper with some momentous story. When the news broke in Washington City that Confederate diplomats James Mason and John Slidell had been captured at sea, Mosby brought the first copy of the *Washington Star* taken from a prisoner. Mosby hoped to give the copy to General Stuart, but he was away, so he gave it to Lieutenant Colonel Fitzhugh Lee, Stuart's second in command. Mosby had no idea that Lee despised him, but he was about to get the message. Fitz was a nephew of Robert E. Lee and an impressive cavalry officer, two years younger than Mosby, but he was a spit-and-polish West Point man, and he disapproved of just about everything about Mosby: the scout used a civilian saddle, wore red artillery facings on his uniform instead of the cavalry buff and, most essential, used irregular tactics. All this was unknown to Mosby, so he proudly reported, "Colonel, here's a copy of today's newspaper." Refusing the paper and staring at Mosby, Fitz replied in an icy tone, "The ruling passion strong in death." Mosby was stunned, as he recognized this phrase from the poem "To Lord Cobham" in Alexander Pope's *Moral Essays*. Cobham was an English religious dissenter hanged and burned in 1417. To Mosby, there could have been no more stinging rebuke than with literature and history, his favorite subjects. Lee was saying that Mosby would get what he deserved when the Yankees shot or hanged him as a spy!

General Stuart respected Fitz Lee, but he disagreed with Lee's antipathy toward irregular warfare and his disapproval of Mosby. Indeed, Stuart saw much of himself in Mosby. Like Mosby, he hated the boredom of inactivity in camp life. Also like Mosby, he abstained from alcohol, never seemed fatigued and could think and act quickly in a crisis. The two men had so much in common that when one described the other, he was in essence describing himself. Stuart realized that the strategic value of cavalry was in reconnaissance and screening, dispelling the fog of war by gathering vital

Confederate cavalry commander James Ewell Brown (Jeb) Stuart, Mosby's mentor for most of the war. *Author's collection.*

information on enemy strength and movement and covering one's own army to deny the enemy such information. He became Robert E. Lee's eyes and ears, one of the best cavalry reconnaissance officers in the war. Stuart had scouted Native Americans out West, and now he was running a scouting school, teaching himself and his men to conduct overnight missions behind enemy lines and use ruses like placing prisoners of war in front of a column to make it appear Union. It was in Fairfax County that Stuart realized he had never seen a scout any better than Mosby.

CHAPTER 3
A Year of Transition

1862

From February 13 to April 23, 1862, Mosby served as adjutant (lieutenant) under Colonel Grumble Jones in the First Virginia Cavalry. He assigned administrative duties to a clerk and, now excused from picket duty, scouted for Stuart. On March 15, Union commander George B. McClellan began secretly moving Union troops to Alexandria and then down to Fort Monroe, at the mouth of the James River, for the Peninsula Campaign to capture Richmond. At the same time, McClellan moved some of his forces toward Manassas. It was not until April 5 that the Confederate high command was sure that the Manassas movement was simply a feint and the Rebel army moved to below the Rappahannock River.

As General Johnston's army moved to the Peninsula to defend Richmond, Stuart's cavalry also moved there. A special election was held on April 23 for Confederate regimental officers. Grumble Jones was voted out, and Fitz Lee was voted in. By that time, Mosby knew that Fitz hated him and would not retain him as adjutant. An hour after the election, Mosby handed Lee his resignation and Lee accepted.

Mosby would never again think of Yorktown without his disappointment in being demoted from a lieutenant to a private. He wrote, "I lost my first commission on the spot where Cornwallis lost his sword." One day later, he met with Stuart, and Jeb made him a courier on his staff. For the next eleven months, Stuart would refer to him as lieutenant or captain, but officially he was a private, which humiliated Mosby.

Mosby continued to read the Richmond newspapers and learned of the Partisan Ranger Act, passed on April 21 by the Confederate Congress.

An Act to organize bands of partisan rangers.
Sec.1. The Congress of the Confederate States of America do enact, That the President be, and he is hereby authorized to commission such officers as he may deem proper with authority to form bands of partisan rangers, in companies, battalions or regiments, to be composed of such members as the President may approve.
Sec. 2. Be it further enacted, That such partisan rangers, after being regularly received in the service, shall be entitled to the same pay, rations, and quarters during their term of service, and be subject to the same regulations as other soldiers.
Sec.3. Be it further enacted, That for any arms and munitions of war captured from the enemy by any body of partisan rangers and delivered to any quartermaster at such place or places as may be designated by a commanding general, the rangers shall be paid their full value in such manner as the Secretary of War may prescribe.
Approved April 21, 1862.

The law authorized the organization of military units to conduct guerrilla warfare behind enemy lines. They were to be part of the army, with the same pay and rations, but as an incentive, the government paid them cash for captured munitions. Mosby decided that partisan life would be for him; he would break away to the Shenandoah Valley and join General Stonewall Jackson as a scout. He was sure Jackson would sponsor him in a partisan operation.

But before this could happen, foundations were laid for the raid that first brought Mosby to prominence. On June 9, Stuart sent out Mosby at the head of four other scouts to check out McClellan's Union forces, which were approaching Richmond. Mosby returned to breathlessly report that McClellan's right wing was unsupported and could easily be penetrated. Mosby wrote the report that Stuart gave to Robert E. Lee as his own. Lee had just been given command of the army, after the wounding of Johnston on May 31 at the battle of Seven Pines. Lee gave permission for a reconnoiter; Stuart took it as the go ahead for his scheme to ride completely around the Union army. Stuart's father-in-law, Philip St. George Cooke, had remained in the Union army and was in command of McClellan's Cavalry Reserve defending the Union rear. Stuart considered Cooke a traitor to Virginia and hoped to embarrass him.

The raid began 2:00 a.m. on June 12, and for three days, Stuart's 1,200 men rode one hundred miles around the Union army as Stuart had dreamed. By the second day, Mosby rode ahead as an advance scout. The only Confederate killed was Captain William Latane. The raid confirmed for Mosby that the life of a partisan was for him. How could anything be this much fun, as he captured and looted Union supply wagons and depots? Mosby loved getting the upper hand on his opponents and seeing the fear in their eyes; finally the weakling was putting the bullies in their place. Stunning and befuddling the foe was more pleasurable than wounding and killing them, and partisan raiding was more profitable than regular warfare. Acquiring and consuming spoils cast a holiday atmosphere on the raid. He took a carpet for Pauline from a Yankee officer's tent. By the end of the raid, he'd gotten two revolvers, a horse and its equipment, totaling $350—more than thirty times a private's $11-per-month salary!

Years later, Mosby would reflect, "The summer sky was a carnival of fun I can never forget. Nobody thought of danger or of sleep...All had perfect confidence in their leader. In the riot among the sutlers' stores 'grim-visaged war had smoothed his wrinkled front,' and Mars resigned his scepter to the jolly god."

The raid also brought him attention. Stuart's report recommended Mosby for a commission, commending him and scout William Farley for their distinguished records of daring and usefulness since the beginning of the war. Lee's congratulatory order mentioned Mosby as one of seven privates who had earned "special commendation" from their commanders. The *Richmond Dispatch* called him "the gallant Lieutenant," even though he was still a private. The *Abingdon Virginian* boasted that Mosby, the local lawyer, "is evidently of the same stuff that [John Hunt] Morgan and [Turner] Ashby and such men are made of."

Mosby met with Stuart and requested a detail of twelve men to go with him for partisan raiding in the rear of the newly designated Union Army of Virginia being organized under General John Pope in Northern Virginia. Pope promised to quell rebellious Virginians by imposing harsh treatment on civilians. As Mosby saw it, Pope "had opened a promising field for partisan warfare and had invited, or rather dared, anybody to take advantage of it." Stuart could not let him go at present, but he promised to send him to Stonewall when the time was right.

Finally, Mosby was given permission and a letter for Jackson. He left Stuart's camp on July 19 with Mortimer Weaver. They rode to Beaver Dam and spent a night with a local farmer. The next day, Mosby sent Weaver ahead

Beaver Dam today. Mosby was captured at this Virginia train station by Union cavalry in July 1862. *Author's collection.*

with his horse; Mosby was going to catch the Virginia Central Railroad to visit his parents, who lived near McIvor's Station along the Orange and Alexandria (O&A) Railroad. Mosby unbuckled his Colt revolvers and placed them in a storage room. As he waited for the train, someone yelled, "Here they come!" Mosby sprang to his feet and saw a regiment of Union cavalry coming at a trot. He was captured, along with his revolvers and Stuart's letter to Jackson. One of the Union cavalrymen wrote an account of the incident that appeared later in a regimental history:

> *During an affray we captured a young Confederate, who gave his name as Captain John S. Mosby. By his sprightly appearance and conversation he attracted considerable attention. He is slight and well formed; has a keen blue eye and a blond complexion, and displays no small amount of Southern bravado in his dress and manners. His gray plush hat is surmounted by a waving plume, which he tosses, as he speaks, in real Prussian style.*

They took him to Fredericksburg and, from there, by steamer to Washington City and the Old Capitol Prison. He had time to read Napoleon's *Maxims*, claiming that he "rather enjoyed my visit to Washington." He spent ten days there and was exchanged under a recently approved cartel of exchange.

He was sent to Hampton Roads on a steamer, which lay anchored for four days before proceeding up the James River. While the other prisoners remained at leisure, he did some scouting and noticed Union transports across the bay. Mosby had become acquainted with the steamer's captain, a Southern man from Baltimore. He asked if the captain could find out where the troops were heading. On the fourth day, he said, "Aquia Creek on the Potomac." Thus Mosby knew that McClellan's drive on Richmond was over and a new Federal advance under General Pope in Northern Virginia was under way.

As soon as the exchange boat arrived at Aiken's Landing, Mosby got permission to go to Lee's headquarters. The general was himself trying to figure out the next move of the Union troops. On August 5, Lee sat down with this dust-covered stranger, who informed him of the Union movements at Hampton Roads. After the war, Mosby would not take part in the worship of Lee, but he regarded Lee as the most impressive person he ever met. He never forgot the awe and veneration he felt in this first meeting. He reminded Lee that he was one of the scouts mentioned in Stuart's report of the ride around McClellan. Lee responded, "Yes, I remember. How did you get gobbled up by those people?" Mosby responded, "I ran, but not as fast as the horses!"

After the war, Mosby claimed that his report sent Stonewall Jackson on his way, bringing on Jackson's victory at the battle of Cedar Mountain. From his solitary point of view it did, but his claim was an exaggeration that failed to take into account the synthesis of intelligence that Lee received from several sources. Still, Mosby's claim calls attention to the long-term value of his report in influencing Lee to have confidence in him as a scout. Mosby's report looked toward a Union advance in Northern Virginia. On August 13 Lee received definite confirmation that McClellan's troops were moving away from the Peninsula. This inaugurated the campaign that culminated with a Confederate victory over Pope's army at Second Manassas (Bull Run), by the end of August.

Remaining with Stuart's cavalry during Second Manassas, Mosby had his horse shot out from under him and a bullet passed through his hat, slightly grazing the top of his skull. At the Battle of Sharpsburg (Antietam), he served as a courier for Stuart, who was screening the far left of the

General Isaac Wistar. Mosby gave water from his canteen to a wounded Colonel Wistar during the Battle of Antietam/ Sharpsburg. They became friends after the war. *Author's collection.*

Confederate line near the West Woods. At about 10:00 a.m., he watched Jackson, "transfigured by the joy of battle," directing his artillery fire against the last Union infantry charge north of Dunkard Church. Stuart saw among the wounded a Confederate lieutenant bending over a Union officer, asking for his formal surrender. Stuart ordered him away. Mosby dismounted, placed a rolled blanket under the man's head and handed him his canteen. Mosby asked his name, and he answered, "Colonel Wistar of the California Regiment." Isaac Jones Wistar recovered and was promoted to brigadier general later that year. After the war, he became president of the Pennsylvania Canal Company, and in 1869, a friend took Mosby to his office in Philadelphia. Mosby identified himself as the private who had given him water at Antietam.

By his twenty-ninth birthday on December 6, 1862, Mosby had been in the Confederate army almost twenty months, and while he had been a first lieutenant and adjutant for less than three months, he was now a private. He had won commendations and praise as a scout for Stuart, who was now a major general and commander of the cavalry of the Army of Northern Virginia. He had made Stuart his latest mentor and had earned his respect and friendship. He had earned the confidence of Lee. But Mosby was extremely dissatisfied. Scouting with the regular cavalry required too many hours of regular camp life and did not provide the emotional satisfaction felt in the practice of irregular warfare. His need for conflict was greater than his need to be Stuart's protégé. As soon as winter postponed regular operations, he asked Stuart again for the loan of a few men, and he would demonstrate he could fight a continual guerrilla war behind enemy lines.

CHAPTER 4

Founding the Partisan Rangers

1863

By December 1862, Washington City was the most heavily fortified capital in the world. Surrounded by a ring of forts and connecting earthworks, it was well suited to defend against a major incursion. Mosby recognized its vulnerability, saying, "A small force, moving with celerity and threatening many points on a line can neutralize a hundred times its own number. The line must be stronger at every point than the attacking force, else it is broken."

When Stuart's cavalry raided into Prince William and Fairfax Counties, on what was known as the Dumfries or Christmas Raid of December 26–31, 1862, Mosby asked Stuart to leave him behind for a few days with nine men. Stuart approved, and Mosby lodged the men in Middleburg, Loudoun County, about twenty miles west of the Union cavalry screen. Mosby knew he had to perform well to continue with an independent command. From Fairfax County, he recruited John Underwood, a man who knew every road and path behind the picket line. He scouted for Mosby for almost a year—his only military experience—until he was killed late in 1863 by a Confederate deserter. Guided by Underwood, Mosby and his men surprised three outposts in two nights, capturing twenty Union cavalrymen and twenty horses. He paroled the soldiers and divided the captured materiel with Underwood and his men. Then Mosby returned with the nine men to Stuart.

Delighted with this result, Stuart detailed fifteen men of the First Virginia Cavalry to Mosby for the winter. Some in camp laughed at Mosby, calling him the "Don Quixote of the War," sure to be captured chasing windmills.

Colonel Sir Percy Wyndham referred to Mosby as a horse thief. The original impetus for the Raid on Fairfax Court House in March 1863 was to capture Sir Percy. *Courtesy of the Library of Congress.*

Mosby first went to Richmond to have a photo taken in a captain's uniform; ever since his demotion in April 1862, he had been known as a lieutenant and captain, but now he would use the title without commission. He took his men to Middleburg and told them to meet at the Mount Zion Church, one mile east of Aldie, on January 26.

Underwood guided them about twelve miles to the picket post at Chantilly Church in Fairfax County, capturing two videttes and ten dismounted men with their horses. Again the prisoners were paroled and the materiel divided. Mosby asked them to tell their commander, Colonel Sir Percy Wyndham, to arm his pickets with Colt revolvers; their obsolete carbines were not worth capturing.

On February 7, Mosby captured several Federal soldiers who were looting local citizens and returned the plunder to its rightful owners. On February 10, Union sergeant James Ames deserted from the Fifth New York Cavalry stationed at Fairfax Court House and joined Mosby's command.

James F. Ames was born in Bangor, Maine. On May 11, 1862, he was promoted to sergeant of Company M Fifth New York Cavalry and transferred to Company L. He was then stationed at Fairfax Court House. After President Lincoln's Emancipation Proclamation took effect on January 1, he deserted, feeling that he could no longer fight for a cause that was fighting for the Negro. He walked south in search of a unit that he had been hearing so much about. That unit was Mosby's Rangers.

When the Rangers first found Ames, they thought him to be a spy and took him to see their commander. He explained to Captain Mosby that he had given up on fighting for the North and wanted to join his unit. Mosby was known for being a good judge of character. After talking to Ames, he felt that he could be trusted.

Ames and Walter Frankland, who had also come to Mosby without a horse, needed to procure a couple mounts. So Ames, along with his comrade, had to walk some thirty miles to Germantown to the camp of the Fifth New York Cavalry. There they were able to walk in past the guards and into the officers' stables, where they saddled up two horses and casually rode out of camp. Since Ames had just left the Fifth New York, he knew the pass signs. This act impressed Mosby's men. He gained the nickname of "Big Yankee" Ames and the trust of Mosby.

On February 11, Mosby's command almost came to an end. He was warned by Laura Ratcliffe of his imminent capture. She was a local young lady who had come to Jeb Stuart's notice when she and her sister attended wounded soldiers after First Manassas. According to several sources, while at the Ratcliffes' home in late December 1862, on a farm just south of the village of Herndon in the Frying Pan area now called Floris, Stuart decided then and there that he was going to let Mosby have a small detachment of men to conduct independent guerrilla operations in Northern Virginia.

A trap had been set for Mosby near Laura's home. A young Union lieutenant could not resist boasting about it to her when he came by to purchase milk, saying, "I know you would give Mosby any information in your possession; but, as you have no horses and the mud is too deep for women folks to walk, you can't tell him; so the next you hear of your 'pet' he will be either dead or our prisoner."

Laura Ratcliffe supplied important information to Mosby and saved his life. *Courtesy of the Stuart-Mosby Cavalry Museum.*

He underestimated her. Laura went out on foot across the fields to reach the home of her cousin George Coleman to ask him to warn Mosby. As luck would have it, her path crossed Mosby's, and she was able to warn him herself, thus saving him from capture. He acknowledged his great debt to her in his memoirs, writing, "I observed two ladies walking rapidly toward me. One was Miss Laura Ratcliffe...But for meeting them, my life as a Partisan would have ended that day."

Mosby avoided the ambush and, in the process, captured a Union sutler's wagon. Captain Willard Glazer, Second New York Cavalry, later described Laura as "a very active and cunning rebel, who is known to our men, and is at least suspected of assisting Mosby not a little in his movements." Glazer further noted that "by the means of Miss Ratcliffe and her rebellious sisterhood, Mosby is generally informed."

The Union's XXII Army Corps consisted of troops engaged in the defenses of Washington City. Brigadier General Edwin H. Stoughton was in command of the Second Brigade of Major General Silas Casey's Division of the XXII Corps. The brigade, consisting of five Vermont infantry regiments, was deployed at outposts in the Centreville-Fairfax area, and Stoughton had his headquarters at Fairfax Court House. Also in the area was a cavalry brigade under the command of Colonel Wyndham. He was a British soldier of fortune who had gained some fame with Garibaldi in Italy and for his luxurious moustache.

During Stonewall Jackson's Valley Campaign of 1862, Wyndham impetuously led his regiment in a charge into Turner Ashby's cavalry, and Wyndham was captured on June 6. He was paroled on August 17. When he returned to duty, he was assigned to command a brigade in Brigadier General George D. Bayard's cavalry division.

Wyndham's brigade included his own First New Jersey Cavalry, the Twelfth Illinois Cavalry, the First Pennsylvania Cavalry and the First Maryland Cavalry. In early 1863, while his brigade was headquartered at Fairfax Court House, Wyndham was given the task of running down Mosby and his guerrillas. Sir Percy did not approve of Mosby's unorthodox tactics and called him a horse thief. Wyndham threatened to burn down towns if their inhabitants did not tell what they knew about Mosby and his men, a policy that did not endear the Englishman to any of the locals.

Mosby began to formulate a bold plan to enter Fairfax Court House and capture Wyndham. Through prisoner interrogations and information from Big Yankee Ames, Mosby learned the locations and strength of the Union outposts in the area, as well as where to find the weak points in the lines. His plan, as he put it, was to "penetrate the outer lines, and go right up to their headquarters and carry off the general commanding and Colonel Wyndham."

Mosby was counting on that very attribute as the key to success. "The safety of the enterprise lay in its novelty; nothing of the kind had been done before," he wrote years later. On the night of March 8, with a light rain falling, Mosby and twenty-nine of his men put the plan into motion. The first step was to pass between the Union encampments at Centreville and Chantilly, without being spotted by Union cavalry. Ames knew where there was a break in the picket lines between the two towns and brought the Rangers through safely without being seen. The first part of the plan was a success; the Union outer perimeter had been breached.

The Rangers proceeded toward Fairfax Court House. Mosby wanted to reach the town by midnight to have sufficient time to complete the mission and return by daybreak. To avoid Union cavalry patrols on the road, the Rangers took to the woods a few miles outside of town and entered Fairfax without incident about 2:00 a.m.

Mosby's men went into action. Guards on duty were taken by surprise and captured. The telegraph operator was seized, and the telegraph wires were cut. A group went to Wyndham's quarters, but he had gone to Washington City that evening. Ames was with this group and captured his former commanding officer, Captain Baker. Others went to the stables and gathered horses. Mosby took five or six of his men and went to General Stoughton's quarters and knocked on the front door.

A window on a floor above opened, and someone asked who was there. Mosby answered, "Fifth New York Cavalry with a dispatch for General Stoughton." Lieutenant Samuel Prentiss, a staff officer, opened the door. "I took hold of his nightshirt, whispered 'I am Mosby' in his ear and told him to take me to General Stoughton's room," Mosby recalled. The officer had little choice and complied.

Stoughton was born in 1838 in Vermont. He graduated from West Point with the class of 1859. By September 1861, he was appointed colonel of the Fourth Vermont Infantry and led his command in the 1862 Peninsula Campaign. Stoughton was only twenty-three years old and said to be the youngest colonel in the army at the time of his appointment.

In November 1862, he was appointed Brigadier General, Volunteers, and assumed command of the Second Vermont Brigade on December 7. Stoughton's brother, Colonel Charles Stoughton, assumed command of the Fourth Vermont Infantry in his stead. Edwin Stoughton's appointment was never confirmed by the U.S. Senate, and it expired March 4, 1863, less than a week before Mosby's Raid.

Stoughton was sleeping soundly when the raiding party entered his room. His mother and sister had been visiting him and had departed just a few hours before. Reportedly, there were empty champagne bottles scattered around the room. "There was no time for ceremony, so I drew up the bedclothes, pulled up the general's shirt, and gave him a spank on his bare back, and told him to get up," Mosby recalled.

Stoughton asked what was going on, to which Mosby replied, "Have you heard of Mosby?"

"Of course I have," sputtered the general. "Have you got him?"

"No, I am Mosby, and he has got you!" The Confederate Ranger added, "Stuart's cavalry has possession of the Court House; be quick and dress." With Mosby and his men pointing their pistols at him, Stoughton got up and dressed. Meanwhile, Mosby took a piece of charred wood and wrote his name on the wall. He wanted to make sure that it was known who was responsible for the deed.

General Edwin Stoughton's capture by Mosby in March 1863 made the Gray Ghost notorious in the North and a hero in the South. *Courtesy of the Library of Congress.*

With Stoughton captured, the raiders prepared to leave. No shots were fired during the raid, and no alarm had been raised, a stroke of luck for the Confederates as they were in the midst of several thousand Union soldiers. But they still had to get back to the Confederate lines. The Rangers had deceived the captured Federals into believing that a much larger Confederate force had swept into town, but as the raiders and their prisoners left town, the actual size of Mosby's force became evident, and prisoners outnumbered their captors. Some prisoners melted into the woods and escaped on the road out of town.

There was a touch of comic opera during the raid. As they were leaving town, an upstairs window of one house was opened, and a man shouted out with authority, asking for the identity of the cavalry. A chorus of laughter from the raiders was the answer. Realizing that it must be an officer of rank, Mosby sent Joseph Nelson and Welt Hatcher to make the capture. Crashing through the front door, they were met by a woman who fought and scratched

General Stoughton's bedroom as it appears today. It is an office for the Truro Episcopal Church in Fairfax, Virginia. *Author's collection.*

until her husband could escape out the back. They searched the house, finding no one, but took his uniform. By it, they knew it was Lieutenant Colonel Robert Johnstone, the cavalry commander. Their prey was hiding in the garden privy until morning. Because of this incident, he gained the odious nickname of "Outhouse" Johnstone.

At 3:30 a.m., the raiding party made its way back, passing close by Federal picket lines but escaping detection. With the telegraph lines cut at Fairfax, no one outside the town knew of the raid, and all the Rangers made it safely back to Confederate lines. In addition to General Stoughton, there were two other officers and thirty enlisted men brought back as prisoners, along with fifty-eight horses.

Mosby's raid, when it became known, was wildly reported in the press. The *New York Times* called the capture "utterly disgraceful." The *Baltimore American* styled Stoughton "the luckless sleeper at Fairfax" who was "Caught

Napping." When President Lincoln was told of the raid, he expressed more concern for the loss of the horses than of his general. Reportedly, he said, "I can make another general with my signature, but it is much more difficult to make horses." It was Lincoln himself who later named Mosby the Gray Ghost. The Union army's biggest fear in Washington City was that Mosby would kidnap Lincoln from right beneath their noses. Lincoln, upon hearing several of his generals discussing Mosby and their fears, loudly announced, "Listen to you men. You speak of Mosby as though he is a ghost, a gray ghost." It wasn't until after the war that Mosby learned of this.

After a brief stop in Warrenton, Mosby and his men took his prisoners to the Confederate cavalry camp at Culpeper Court House, where Stoughton was turned over to his West Point classmate General Fitzhugh Lee. Mosby proclaimed, "General, here is your friend General Stoughton, whom I have just captured with his staff at Fairfax Court House." Astonished, Lee looked icily at Mosby and then jumped to his feet and shook Stoughton's hand and invited him to have a seat by the fire to dry out from the ride in the cold rain. Mosby was dripping wet and cold as well, but Lee just stared at him as though he should leave. "It was plain he was sorry for what I had done," Mosby later wrote. "I was very mad at such treatment."

Ignoring Lee, Mosby shook hands with Stoughton and left.

General Stuart's reaction greatly contrasted with Fitz Lee. Stuart issued an order commending Mosby for "boldness, skill, and success" and "daring enterprise and dashing heroism" in several forays. On March 19, Robert E. Lee, who had commended "Lieutenant Mosby" on February 28 for capturing many prisoners and boldly harassing the enemy, had him appointed captain of Partisan Rangers, effective March 15, and, within another week, promoted him to major, effective March 26. Mosby's appointment as an officer was only temporary until he could recruit a company to be mustered into the regular cavalry. Lee thought he was doing best, for troops operating under the term "partisan" had a reputation for pillaging farms and terrorizing local citizens. Stuart agreed with Lee and advised Mosby, "By all means ignore the term 'Partisan Ranger.' It is in bad repute. Call your command 'Mosby's Regulars.'"

Mosby went against both their advice and public opinion—he wanted a company of Rangers, not Regulars. He wrote to Stuart that he could not accept the appointment on Lee's terms, saying that his men had joined him under the impression that they would be entitled to spoils under the Partisan Ranger Act. He demanded the authority to enroll his men as partisans.

Aiding him in his campaign to remain a partisan was the capture of Stoughton, which had made him famous and a hero of the Southern people.

Fitzhugh Lee, Confederate cavalry commander and nephew of Robert E. Lee. He could not stand Mosby's non-adherence to army regulation. *Courtesy of the Library of Congress.*

"Your praise is on every lip," Stuart wrote. The *Richmond Enquirer* published Stuart's commendation and a letter from Mosby describing the raid, and the editors praised him as a "gallant Captain" who had performed a "brilliant act." "Capture of a Yankee Brigadier," ran the headline in the *Richmond Dispatch*, and the front-page report stated that Mosby rousted thirty men, a captain and the general from their beds.

Not resting on his laurels, Mosby next led his men in the Saint Patrick's Day Raid on March 17. Mosby and forty of his men moved against the twenty-five-man picket post of the First Vermont Cavalry at Herndon Station, nine miles north of Fairfax Court House. They entered the village at noon from the north, the time and direction for the guards to change. The guards believed they were a Union relief party. Mosby and his men captured the vidette without a shot and then charged a dismounted Union lieutenant and his men. They ran into a sawmill. Mosby demanded their surrender or he would fire the building. They quickly acquiesced. At a nearby house, the

Raiders noticed four officers' horses tethered outside. Inside the house, they found dinner set, but no apparent diners. Ames located a small door, which led to an overhead garret. He kicked in the door and demanded for anyone there to come out. Receiving no reply, he fired a shot into the darkness, resulting in three Union officers surrendering. They were soon joined by a fourth companion, who fell through the plaster of the ceiling. They had been a Union cavalry investigating committee having lunch. They were there to look into charges that Yankee pickets were stealing from civilians. One member was Major William Wells, who later became a general. Mosby's report, which Lee passed on to President Jefferson Davis, stated, "I brought off 25 prisoners—a major, 1 captain, 2 lieutenants, and 21 men, all their arms, 26 horses and equipments...My loss was nothing." "Still Gobbling Them Up," reported the *Washington Star*. The picket curtain was pulled back from Dranesville and Herndon to Difficult Run.

Giving his men six days rest, Mosby met with them at Rector's Cross Roads on March 23. He decided on a daylight raid on the Fifth New York Cavalry at Chantilly. He hoped to slip through the same fields that he had used in the Stoughton Raid and approach Chantilly from the rear. Fifty-five men showed up, which was enough to have attracted unwanted attention, but Mosby accepted them all—he was in no position to turn them away.

They traveled twenty-three miles, and by the time they reached Chantilly, the horses were jaded. Mosby saw his mistake in not arriving with fresh horses. Two videttes spotted the raiders and spread the alarm to Chantilly. Mosby cancelled the raid, but seven or eight of his men attacked an advanced Union picket, killing one and capturing six. Then they watched as about seventy men of the Fifth New York saddled up and headed toward them.

Mosby realized they were in great danger because of the Union's fresh horses and his exhausted ones. He knew that if he retreated they would overtake and stampede his men. So he decided on an ancient tactic known as "fake retreat." He went three miles west of Chantilly, near woods where Union troops had erected an abatis, or barricade of fallen trees. Here Mosby halted, sending five of his men home with the seven prisoners, and ordered the others to draw sabers and prepare to charge. When the enemy was within a hundred yards, he ordered the charge. Taken by surprise, the Federals halted, but before they could wheel, Mosby's men were among them. In the melee, sabers were returned to their scabbards and revolvers drawn.

The result was three dead Union cavalrymen, one mortally wounded and thirty-six captured, including one lieutenant, as well as fifty horses. "Hurrah for Mosby!" Lee exclaimed, "I wish I had a hundred like him."

Mosby had turned a potential defeat into a rout of the enemy by using a mounted countercharge from ambush and melee with revolvers. His maxim henceforth would be to never stand still and receive a charge but always take the offensive. He had learned the uselessness of the saber against the revolver and not to make contact with the enemy when his horses were jaded.

In three months as leader of an independent command, Mosby had forced major rearrangements on the early-warning screen in Washington's defenses, he had attracted forty temporary volunteers to reinforce his fifteen men on loan from Stuart, he had created fear in the enemy minds, he had become a Southern hero and he had learned valuable tactical lessons. He had moved up from private to major, but he still had to convince Stuart and Lee to give him and his men permanent status as Partisan Rangers. He had no knowledge of it at the time but learned later that he had a silent admirer high in the Confederate government—Secretary of War James A. Seddon, who was reading his reports and cheering to himself. Eventually Seddon would overrule Stuart and Lee and, in spite of the negative reputation of Rangers in general, would give Mosby what he needed.

On the afternoon of March 31, Mosby and about seventy of his Rangers set out from Rectortown in Fauquier County toward Fairfax County through snow and rain. Their destination was Dranesville, near the Loudoun-Fairfax border. They planned on attacking the Union garrison stationed there, which was often sent into Loudoun and Fauquier Counties to raid. Unfortunately for the Rangers, they were foiled by their own success.

Upon arriving in Dranesville, they found the garrison abandoned, having been pulled back east of Difficult Run in the face of mounting pressure from the Partisan warfare being waged by Mosby. With night fast approaching, the Rangers set out back west into Loudoun, eventually stopping at the farm of Thomas and Lydia Miskel at about 10:00 p.m. to get forage for their mounts and rest for the night. At the farm, located on the eastern bank of Broad Run near its confluence with the Potomac River, a few miles north of the Leesburg Pike, the Rangers felt safe from Federal patrols. Most of the Rangers tied their mounts in the barnyard and made their beds in the barn, which was surrounded by a high fence with only a single gate opening out to the lane running to the road to Leesburg Pike. The lane, in turn, was bounded on both sides by two fences. Mosby and his officers took refuge in the main house.

The presence of Mosby and his Rangers was a conspicuous sight to the locals, who knew all too well what the Federals might do to them if they were found aiding and abetting the Rangers. Thus, a local woman made her way to the Federal lines at Union Church, arriving around midnight. She reported

General Robert E. Lee, portrayed in the *Illustrated London News* in 1863. *Author's collection.*

Mosby's presence to Major Charles F. Taggart of the Second Pennsylvania Cavalry. Upon learning the news, Taggart immediately dispatched Captain Henry C. Flint and five companies of the First Vermont Cavalry to kill or capture the Rangers.

By early dawn of April 1, the Federals had reached Broad Run on the Pike and stopped briefly at a house to inquire as to the whereabouts of the Miskel Farm. They then set out toward the farm and Mosby's unsuspecting men. As fate would have it, Ranger Dick Moran had been in the house the Federals stopped at, visiting friends. As soon as the Federals left, he mounted his horse and took off across the fields to warn Mosby and his fellow Rangers.

As Captain Flint approached the Miskel Farm, he divided his command, assigning Captain George H. Bean command of a fifty-man reserve force while he maintained command of the vanguard. Bean was detailed with the duty of barricading the barnyard gate after Flint and his men went through and then circling around behind the barn to cut off all routes of escape for the Rangers. Just as Flint prepared to attack, Moran came rushing by and burst into the barnyard yelling for his comrades to mount up and prepare to give fight. The Rangers rushed to their mounts, and Mosby burst from the main house as the Federals charged into the barnyard. Though armed with carbines, Flint opted for the romance of a cavalry charge and ordered his men to unsheathe their sabers.

As the Federals fell upon the Rangers, they were met with a sharp volley of pistol fire from the partially mounted Confederates. Flint was killed instantly, struck by six bullets, and fell from his horse. At this point, the Federal attack broke down, and the men began to panic as they struggled to break through the locked gate. Among the first to make it through the gate was Bean, who, after Flint died, was supposed to be in command. Mosby seized the initiative and led a counterattack with the twenty or so Rangers that had been able to mount up. The Rangers were on top of the Federals, who were trapped in the barnyard lane, causing the vast majority to surrender. Those who managed to escape were pursued for several miles by the victorious Rangers.

When the smoke cleared, Mosby had suffered one killed and three wounded. The Rangers killed nine, including Flint and another officer; wounded fifteen, including three officers; and captured eighty-two. In addition, ninety-five horses were seized by the Rangers. The fight resulted in a crushing defeat for the Federals; they had the Rangers bottled up in a barnyard with only one exit, on a farm surrounded on two sides by water and outnumbered them by more than two to one. By all accounts, the Rangers should have been wiped out that morning, but Flint made several mistakes. The most glaring was his insistence on leading a saber charge against the Rangers, who made notorious use of drawn pistols in their fights. The Vermonters were armed with carbines, which the Rangers could not match. If Flint had dismounted and attacked with those weapons, the Federals could have easily overpowered the trapped Rangers and, in all likelihood, Flint would have survived the fight rather than running head-on into the Rangers' deadly volley.

Flint's second mistake was dividing his unit and placing Bean as second in command. What knowledge Flint had of Bean's leadership qualities is unknown, but even after Flint had been killed, the Federals still had the Rangers surrounded and outnumbered. A competent officer could have rallied the unit and pressed the attack; instead, Bean led the retreat. For his incompetence and cowardice, Bean was subsequently drummed from the service. This Fight at Miskel Farm taught Mosby and his troops many valuable lessons, two of which being that he would never again put himself in such a vulnerable position or leave himself encamped without the protection of pickets.

Seeing the power of the Colt revolver in this second melee against the saber, Mosby would also never again order a saber charge. He had carried a Colt since before First Manassas but had not realized its power until Chantilly and this fight. His characteristic tactic became the mounted charge, given increased shock and killing power by replacing the saber with two or more Colt revolvers per man. These guns used paper cartridges and percussion caps, so they had to be loaded ahead of time. As the saying went, "God created man, and Sam Colt made them equal." Mosby said the saber was as out-of-date as a coat of mail, as worthless as a cornstalk and good for nothing but roasting meat over a fire. To attack with a saber, you had to get close enough to strike the enemy; to hit an opponent with a .36- or .44-caliber six-shooter, you had to be within thirty feet. By coming into close quarters in order to use their sabers, the Union cavalry were playing Mosby's game—coming within range of his pistols.

Within a single month, and not yet thirty years old, Mosby had become immortal. From the moment he had awakened Stoughton, he was one of the most famous soldiers in America. The Fairfax Raid became his signature incident. It is cited prominently in every Mosby memoir and biography. It is the subject of the first episode of the *Gray Ghost* television series in 1957, the centerpiece of the Walt Disney 1967 film *Mosby's Marauders* and the subject of a chapter, "A Gray Ghost Captures a General," in a 1998 volume, *Daring Raiders*. The Stoughton Raid appears in the companion to the Ken Burns *Civil War* documentaries and in the History Channel's *Civil War Journal*: "The Gray Ghost—John Singleton Mosby."

Mosby spent the next month testing the Federal cavalry screen in Northern Virginia and making a few runs into the Shenandoah Valley near Winchester. Early on the morning of May 3, he and one hundred men attacked a small detachment of Union infantry guarding the railroad near Warrenton Junction. He captured a few men and learned of a small cavalry camp nearby. He decided to blindly attack the camp. At about 9:00 a.m., with the roar of cannon in the Battle of Chancellorsville in the distance, Mosby charged the

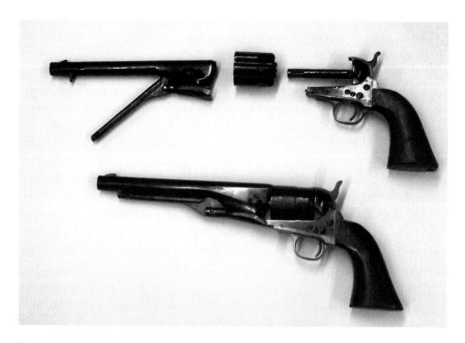

The Army Colt 1860 series revolver, the preferred offensive weapon of Mosby's Rangers. *Author's collection.*

camp of the First Virginia Union Cavalry. As they were surrendering, down the track came two hundred of the Fifth New York and First Vermont Cavalry, with sabers drawn. Their camp was only one mile northeast, and they had heard the pistol shots. Mosby ordered a countercharge à la Chantilly, but his men ignored him and fled in panic. What became known as the Warrenton Junction Raid was his first defeat—he lost three dead, seventeen wounded and six captured. But he learned from this experience and always scouted before any future enemy encounter.

At that time, he returned the original fifteen men lent to him by Stuart. At an assembly called for May 10, only thirty-seven showed up. They cut telegraph wires and set fire to the small railroad bridges at Kettle Run and Cedar Run. Union infantry put out the Kettle Run blaze before it caused serious damage. Since no spoils were taken, his men called the raid a failure. Mosby realized that to keep his men, he had to supply them with spoils. For them, war did not mean fighting for some abstract idea; it meant prisoners, arms, horses and sutlers' stores. Because of this, on May 19, Mosby asked Stuart for the use of a mountain rifle with which he could attack a train and provide spoils for his men. Stuart warned him not to attack near a Union cavalry camp.

On May 27, Mosby received the cannon, and Sam Chapman drilled some of the men in its use. Mosby realized later that what he was doing was not only hazardous but also foolhardy. The cannon changed the nature of his guerrilla operations. For one thing, it attracted attention and violated his rule of keeping his headquarters in the saddle. The local Union commander, Colonel William D. Mann of the Seventh Michigan Cavalry, learned about it from his scouts. It was a small mountain rifle and was light for fast travel, with no caisson and only fifteen rounds of ammunition in the limber chest, plenty to stop a train but not enough for a skirmish. Now Mosby could no longer run from a superior force but would have to defend the cannon. He would have needed two hundred well-organized cavalry to defend the gun instead of the forty-eight conglomerates that showed up. With this small, unorganized force, the cannon was a millstone around his neck.

Early on the morning of May 30, Mosby and his Rangers marched briskly to Catlett's Station on the O&A Railroad. They cut telegraph wire, unfastened the track and attached a wire to pull the track out of line when the engine came along, therefore throwing the train off the track. Soon, the train came but stopped abruptly when reaching the dangerous rail. The rifle was used to fire a shot into the engine. The Rangers charged the infantry guarding the train. The Yankees ran, leaving the train in the Partisans' hands. Hearing the guns and seeing the smoke of the burning train, Colonel Mann ordered the Fifth New York Cavalry to intercept Mosby while Mann took the First Vermont Cavalry and his Seventh Michigan Cavalry along the railroad line toward the disabled train. Mosby saw them coming at his front and had his gun spit a shell into the enemy's ranks to check their advance for a moment. Then Mosby stood and fought, dispersing the Federals twice—first with cannon fire, and then with a cavalry charge. The large number of Union cavalry and exhaustion of ammunition eventually caused Mosby to retreat and abandon the cannon after desperate hand-to-hand combat. The Federals, with four killed and fifteen wounded, did not pursue Mosby. Mosby's loss was painful—five killed, twenty wounded and ten prisoners taken.

The *Richmond Dispatch* ran the headline "Mosby Again at Work" and praised him for defending the cannon (even though he had lost it). He had learned that capturing trains was complicated and having a cannon required highly organized and disciplined men. The *New York Times* commended the Union cavalry for giving "the guerrilla chieftain the soundest thrashing he has yet received." The captured cannon was polished and placed in front of Union cavalry headquarters at Fairfax Court House.

The Hathaway House today. Mosby had one of his narrow escapes from Union cavalry hiding in a tree close to this residence. *Author's collection.*

Mosby made another exception to his rule of having headquarters in the saddle by sending for his wife and children to join him in Fauquier County. On March 16, he had written Pauline that he had arranged room and board with James and Elizabeth Hathaway. They had a large plantation (760 acres and thirty-one slaves) and a three-story brick house about five miles north of Salem in the heart of Mosby's Confederacy. Fount Beattie was boarding there and eventually would marry one of Hathaway's daughters, Anne, producing twelve children. Pauline, along with their children, May and Bev, arrived, and her third child may have been conceived there, born on December 8 and named John S. Mosby Jr.

One of Mosby's close escapes happened in May, when he was getting a haircut and shave in Warrenton. The town was surrounded by Northern troops and no one expected him. There was a sudden commotion as Union cavalry came riding through town. The quick-thinking barber lathered Mosby's face. A Yankee lieutenant entered the shop and questioned Mosby, who gave him a false name. The Yankees missed their chance to capture the Gray Ghost.

Mosby's partisan career almost came to an end at the Hathaway residence on June 8. At 8:00 p.m., Captain William Boyd and a detachment of the First New York Cavalry were scouting in Salem, when someone told him that Mosby was staying at the Hathaways. They surrounded the house about midnight. They found Pauline and the children in an upstairs bedroom, but no sign of Mosby. They took James Hathaway as prisoner, along with some of the horses, including Mosby's, which they renamed "Lady Mosby." If they had only searched the large tree close to the house, they might have discovered Mosby hiding in one of the limbs. During the confusion, Mosby had climbed out just before the Federals entered the house.

Two days after the Hathaway Raid, Mosby was finally able to form his Partisan Rangers. Both Lee and Stuart had turned him down, but he continued to have a supporter in Seddon. He had been against partisans before Mosby went independent. However, Seddon kept reading Mosby's reports and found that Mosby was boarding his men in homes and not permanent camps, disbanding and reassembling them in the manner of a classic people's war. Going against his own rule, he gave Mosby authority to recruit a new Ranger command. He stated that Mosby's commission as captain of Rangers implied the authority to organize a company of Rangers, and Lee and Stuart acquiesced.

So Mosby met with his command on June 10 near Rector's Cross Roads and was organized for the first time as Company A, Forty-third Battalion Partisan Rangers. The law required Mosby to allow the men of the company to elect their officers. But he remembered what this provision had done earlier in the war to him and Grumble Jones, and he realized that combining democracy with discipline was "as dangerous as adding acid to alkali." Throughout the war, he would appoint all of his officers and force the men to approve. He would draw the company up, nominate an officer, call for 'ayes' and quickly declare unanimity. Once, when the men grumbled against what they called "Mosby elections," he nominated a man and declared that anyone who disagreed should step forward and he would send them to the regular army. No one did, and he declared the candidate elected.

The very next day, Mosby took one hundred men, including thirty Prince William County Rangers under Captain William G. Brawner, on a raid into Maryland at Seneca Mills, about twenty miles north of Washington City. They attacked and routed eighty men of the Sixth Michigan Cavalry, plundering and burning their camp, seizing their colors and capturing seventeen men and thirty horses. Two of Mosby's men were killed, including Captain Brawner. Mosby sent the captured flag on to Stuart. Endorsing his

At Rector's Cross Roads, Mosby officially formed the Forty-third Virginia Cavalry Battalion in June 1863. Many of his raids started from this point. *Author's collection.*

report, Stuart recommended Mosby's promotion to lieutenant colonel. With his new authority, Mosby found it easier to order and maintain his attack and enforce discipline during the looting and retreat.

On June 17, Mosby hoped for another raid into Maryland. But seeing the Union army moving toward Fairfax to shadow Lee and the Rebel army into Maryland, Mosby struck on a plan to capture couriers and stragglers. He cancelled the raid and took three men and rode toward the camp of General George G. Meade's V Corps at Gum Springs, about six miles east of Aldie and fell in with the stream of wagons and troops moving west along the Little River Turnpike. In the darkness, their gray uniforms were indistinguishable from blue. They stopped at the front gate of Almond Birch's home, a Union sympathizer, and saw an orderly holding the bridles of three horses. Pretending to be a Union officer, he asked the man whose horses they were, and he reported that they belonged to Major Sterling and Captain Fisher of General Hooker's headquarters with dispatches, inside having supper. Mosby called him over, leaned down, grabbed him by the collar and whispered, "You are my prisoner. My name is Mosby." Soon the officers came out and were captured, and Mosby relieved them of a satchel of letters. Major William R. Sterling was a member of Hooker's general staff, and Captain Benjamin F. Fisher was the chief acting signal officer.

Mosby took the prisoners and letters to a friendly farmhouse. The letters contained Hooker's correspondence to General Alfred Pleasonton, the Union cavalry commander at Aldie. The letters verified that Hooker had no idea where Lee was and that he was sending out cavalry patrols, which Stuart could now counter. They also gave the number of divisions in Hooker's army, enabling Lee and Stuart to estimate their strength. Once again, Mosby had proved invaluable as a scout.

Stuart's report on the Gettysburg Campaign commended Mosby for capturing the dispatches and for scouting reports that informed him of enemy movements. "In this difficult search, the fearless and indefatigable Major Mosby was particularly active and efficient. His information was always accurate and reliable." In the nine days from June 16 to June 24, Mosby scouted behind the lines for Stuart five times, activities that involved him in Stuart's decision to ride around the Union army on the march to Gettysburg. By June 28, General Meade was given command of the Union army, taking over for Hooker.

Sent out by Stuart on his fifth scout on June 23, Mosby came upon two Union cavalrymen picking cherries near Frying Pan. He drew his revolver under his gum cloth and asked what regiment they belonged to. He then drew out his pistol and told them his name was Mosby. He observed that the name seemed to put them under a spell. On his way back to Stuart, he found the turnpike blocked by a Union wagon train, with a strong cavalry escort. He decided to ride along, hoping to be mistaken for a Union officer. He later admitted that it was the greatest risk he ever took in the war. For two hundred yards he continued with the train, with his pistol under his cape, trained on his prisoners. He turned left on the nearest road and crossed the mountains, paroling his prisoners but keeping their horses.

On the morning of June 24, Mosby reported to Stuart that Hooker's army had not moved, and he could pass through his corps and enter Maryland at Seneca Ford. Stuart asked Mosby to meet him the next morning ten miles east of Aldie to guide the way. However, that next morning when Mosby got to the meeting place, he found Hooker's army moving toward the Potomac. Hearing artillery firing in the distance, Mosby assumed that it must have been Stuart, who had also ran into the Union forces and was heading back toward the Valley to link up with Lee. He had no idea that Stuart would continue his ride around the Union army. Mosby's judgment was so sure that Stuart had turned back that he did not even go looking for him. After the war, Lee supporters condemned Stuart for disobeying Lee's orders by not turning back after meeting a hindrance. But Lee had clearly left it up to Stuart to judge whether there was a hindrance. Stuart was not guilty of disobeying orders; he was guilty only of a mistake in judgment, one that Mosby did not make that day.

Mosby dispersed his men and on June 28 came together with thirty men at Upperville. They went through Snicker's Gap into the Shenandoah Valley and crossed the Potomac River near Hancock, Maryland, on July 1 and raided Mercersburg, Pennsylvania. As they crossed the Mason-Dixon Line, Big Yankee Ames said, "Well, I am going with you, but I will not fire a shot. When the Emancipation Proclamation was issued and I saw it was a war for the black man and not for the Union, I joined the South and am willing to fight to repel the invasion of her soil, and am willing to give my life in her defense, but I will not fight on Northern soil."

They captured 218 cattle and 15 horses and returned to Virginia.

Since his capture of General Stoughton, Mosby had learned several important lessons. He recognized the superiority of the revolver over the saber in a mounted charge and melee. He had learned to arrive at the objective with rested horses, scout before attacking and avoid bivouacking in a cul-de-sac. What he had known all along about his men demanding spoils had been confirmed, and he realized what Stuart meant when he warned him to avoid raiding near strong enemy cavalry camps to allow his men time to plunder. He learned what having a cannon meant. Now that he was organized under the Partisan Ranger Act, he had authority over his command and could exert his special style of leadership.

Mosby's primary contribution to cavalry tactics was the importance of the mounted charge. After the war, he wrote, "It was a rule from which I never departed, not to stand still and receive a charge, but always to act on the offensive." He always attempted to begin a charge by ordering the men into a column of fours, and it was an honor to be selected to ride in the front rank of four. Then he would silently signal or yell, "Boys, go through 'em!" and the race started with each man for himself, spurring his mount and holding the bridle reins in one hand or dropping them and firing a revolver in each hand. Standard cavalry tactics required staying in line in correct alignment, which was impossible to use against Mosby. "The enemy was amidst the men," reported one Union commander, "and both parties were so mixed up that it was impossible to get the men into line."

Mosby scheduled no target practice, but his men frequently trained on their own, with the goal of hitting a tree trunk three times when riding by in a full run. "My men had no superiors in the saddle and were expert pistol shots," he said. Since the Colt was accurate only for ten yards, he ordered them to hold their fire until they could distinguish the eyes of an opponent. The enemy using sabers cooperated by closing to arm-and-blade length, and sometimes after a fight, men gathering up wounded and dead noticed powder burns on their uniforms. He and his men attempted to wound or kill the enemy commander in the first contact to cause loss of confidence and demoralization. On their own, after using all of their bullets, some men would pistol-whip the enemy with empty revolvers.

Mosby recognized that his men would fight this way if he followed one of the cardinal rules of irregular warfare, the principle that there were no rules. He enjoyed casting aside the narrow, rigid rules of the military manuals. He never blinked at disobeying regulations forbidding him to recruit eligible conscripts or requiring officer elections. Instead he concentrated on factors that were vital to success such as spoils, continued civilian support, accurate intelligence and irregular tactics. Civilians assisted him in maintaining discipline by applying social pressure, but the operation depended on his strength of character and leadership ability. It is amazing that he led his men for the first five months with no organization whatsoever and continued for almost two more years with no training cycle and no military courtesy and only his own personal discipline. Elsewhere in the South the amount of freedom allowed partisans broke down in indolence and brigandage. Mosby admonished, "We did not drill ourselves into a machine that could not operate when any part went wrong. We just maintained our individuality and at the same time a cohesiveness and went to the task."

After the Battle of Gettysburg, Meade brought the Union army back into Northern Virginia. He carefully guarded his main supply line on the O&A Railroad but, for a few weeks, provided no escort for sutlers coming from Washington City on the Warrenton Turnpike. Less than seven miles into Virginia, the merchants came to a cavalryman standing in the road beckoning them to turn into a bypath; it was Mosby in broad daylight directing traffic from both directions into a ravine where his men were waiting to unhitch the horses and plunder the goods. One warm day, dressed in a shirt and blue trousers, he rode into a sutler's camp and ordered a beer and a slice of cake. From the unsuspecting sutler he obtained intelligence useful for locating that day's roadblock. In two weeks with thirty men, he captured at least 118 sutler and army wagons, adventures dramatized on the stage in Alexandria as *The Guerilla; or, Mosby in Five Hundred Sutler-wagons.*

Stuart approved, but Lee questioned whether Mosby was giving too much attention to spoils and neglecting military objectives. Gaining spoils was at the heart of Mosby's operation and the basic motivator in the Partisan Ranger Act. In the American Revolution, Thomas Sumter, under Sumter's Law, allowed his men to keep plunder from the enemy. Originally from Virginia, Sumter settled in South Carolina before the Revolution. In February 1776, Sumter was elected lieutenant colonel of the Second Regiment of the South Carolina Line, of which he was later appointed colonel. He subsequently was appointed brigadier general of the South Carolina militia, a post he held until the end of the war. He participated in several battles in the early months of the war, including the campaign to prevent an invasion of Georgia. Perhaps his greatest military achievement was his partisan campaigning, which contributed to Lord Cornwallis's decision to leave the Carolinas for Virginia, where he was defeated at Yorktown in October 1781. Sumter acquired the nickname "the Carolina Gamecock" during the American Revolution for his fierce fighting tactics, regardless of his size. A British general commented that Sumter "fought like a gamecock," and Cornwallis paid him the finest tribute when he described the Gamecock as his greatest plague. Fort Sumter in Charleston Harbor was named for him.

The Confederate Partisan Ranger Act made keeping plunder legal through government reimbursement. The Confederate Congress sought to encourage Partisans by applying the principal of maritime prize law, without the procedure of condemning the seized property in prize court. Like privateering, the act harnessed avarice for the cause. The law, its regulations and practices authorized payment for captured arms and munitions, infantry and cavalry accoutrements, horses, mules and cattle. Beef cattle were turned over to the commissary and other items to any quartermaster.

After a raid, Mosby would sometimes award the best horses to men who had acted with uncommon bravery, and the remainder was divided by lottery among the men who had participated in the raid. The men then sold the extra horses to the quartermaster. In 1863, the government paid $110 for a cavalry horse; a revolver was worth a minimum of $12, a rifle $10. Therefore, a Mosby raider could earn more than $130 by capturing one Union cavalryman. This was twelve months' pay for a private. The Confederate government paid in gold and greenbacks, protecting Mosby and others from the depredations of inflation suffered by Confederates in general.

By the middle of August, the U.S. War Department finally awakened to the plight of the sutlers going between Alexandria and Warrenton. Thus, convoys

Revolutionary War general Thomas Sumter, the South Carolina Gamecock, one of the models for Mosby's Partisan Rangers. *Author's collection.*

left Washington City on Mondays at 9:00 a.m. and returned from Warrenton Junction on Thursdays at 9:00 a.m. On August 21, Meade complained to Halleck that his cavalry was as exhausted as if they were in active operations because they had to protect his flanks and long line of supply.

When Lee received Mosby's August 4 report, with Stuart's favorable endorsement, there was a false rumor circulating that Mosby had held an auction in Charlottesville and sold $30,000 worth of spoils. Lee did endorse

Mosby's report, commending him for "boldness and good management," but he was concerned that he was taking too few men on his raids and giving too much attention to merchants and not enough to military targets. At the same time, Lee sent a letter to Stuart, stating that Mosby had a large number of men but only used a few on his raids and directing Stuart to order Mosby to keep his men on duty, hold no more auctions and attack enemy outposts and communications, especially the O&A Railroad, which would divert troops to the rear and weaken the Union army.

Stuart had a deeper appreciation of guerrilla warfare than Lee, and he was unconcerned. He realized that attacking unguarded sutler wagons was part of hitting the enemy where it was weak and harassing it like a gnat. Lee's reprimand also warned Mosby that Lee failed to appreciate the principle that a force of a few men using stealth can operate more effectively in hit-and-run raids than a large force. Mosby felt indignant that Lee assumed that the auction rumor was true without inquiring, and Lee was misinformed on how few men he had. During this period, Mosby had no more than eighty men and usually used only thirty at a time.

On August 24, Mosby took thirty of his men to burn some railroad trestles in obedience to Lee's command. They were hiding in the woods a short distance from Billy Gooding's Tavern, three miles east of Fairfax Court House, in Annandale, when a drove of one hundred Union cavalry horses were being guarded by twenty-five members of the Second Massachusetts Cavalry. This was too good to be true, so Mosby decided to take the horses and burn the bridges later. While the Union men were watering their horses, Mosby and his men attacked from both sides. Meanwhile, a party of nine from the Thirteenth New York Cavalry happened to increase Union strength. Several Federals used their revolvers, and a few fired from windows of the tavern. But Mosby's men had momentum and a crossfire. After a brief, sharp fight, all the Union men ran away or surrendered. Mosby's men captured twelve prisoners and eighty-five horses. The Union had two dead and five wounded; Mosby had two dead and three wounded, including himself.

One bullet pierced his side and passed around his ribs, and the other went through his right thigh, killing his horse. Fortunately, neither bullet hit a vital organ or a bone. Wisely, Mosby had recruited Dr. William L. Dunn as assistant surgeon of the command. Dr. Dunn and three men took him to a nearby pine woods, where Dunn immediately treated the wounds. Before being taken away, Mosby ordered Lieutenant William T. Turner to take a few men and burn the trestles. They managed to burn one. A few days later, some of the men took Mosby to Idle Wilde, his parents' home near Lynchburg, to recuperate.

GOODING'S TAVERN

The Gooding Tavern served Little River Turnpike travelers and stagecoach passengers from 1807-1879 and was famous for "the best fried chicken" and "peaches and honey." For the community, the tavern served as a social and commercial gathering place. The Goodings also operated a blacksmith shop and stable. Several Civil War skirmishes occurred around the tavern. On 24 August 1863, Confederate partisan ranger Major John S. Mosby was severely wounded by the Union 2nd Massachusetts Cavalry. Two of his officers were killed and three men wounded. Union losses included two killed, three wounded and nine prisoners taken. The tavern burned down in 1879.

THE FAIRFAX COUNTY HISTORY COMMISSION, 2011

Mosby was seriously wounded at Gooding's Tavern. The historical marker is across from the entrance to Northern Virginia Community College in Annandale, Virginia. *Author's collection.*

The Union cavalrymen who escaped reported that Mosby was wounded, perhaps mortally, and a rumor started that he was dead. On August 29, the *Washington Star* published a report that a woman in Upperville had seen Mosby coming through in a guarded wagon with "the ghastly hue of death upon him." Then on August 31, the *New York Herald* reported that he had died three days before in Dranesville and ran his obituary, titled, "Sketch of Mosby, Guerilla Chief." But by September 8, the *Herald* correspondent in Washington City admitted that it was actually impossible to know whether he was alive or dead.

When Mosby was nearly recovered, he went to Richmond to meet with Secretary of War Seddon. He was appreciative of Seddon's approval of his partisan status. Seddon said that he had read all of Mosby's reports and spoke in the highest terms of the service of Mosby's command. Next he visited Lee at his headquarters at Orange Court House. It was just their second meeting, and it helped that Mosby was injured. Lee treated him kindly and said he was greatly satisfied with Mosby's conduct. He apologized for jumping to a conclusion on the rumor of the Charlottesville "auction." Then they discussed how to disrupt the O&A Railroad and the capture of prominent Union officials.

Upon returning to duty on September 21, Mosby took forty men to disrupt the O&A near Warrenton Junction. He left the majority in a nearby wood and took three men to scout the railroad tracks. Instead of a train, he saw a heavily guarded mule wagon train headed toward Meade with pontoon bridges. Mosby saw that Meade was planning to cross the Rapidan River and flank Lee's army. He sent a message by courier to Stuart, and Stuart reported it to Lee. Meade canceled the plan, and the report had no strategic impact, but once again Mosby had provided potentially valuable intelligence.

After several raids in the Manassas Junction and Burke Station areas, Mosby took eight of his men closer into Alexandria. He was scouting as preparation to follow Lee's other instructions—the capture of Union officials. On September 27, he returned to Fairfax County and slept in the pines between Fairfax Court House and Alexandria. The next day, he captured six stragglers and sent them off guarded by four of his men. With the other four, after dark, he penetrated the ring of capital defenses and entered Alexandria to capture Lincoln's man in Virginia, the "Father" of West Virginia and now "Restored Governor" of Federal-controlled Virginia (which at that point included Arlington, Alexandria and parts of Fairfax County), Francis H. Pierpont.

Pierpont had led the movement for the creation of West Virginia and, when statehood was achieved in 1863, had moved to Alexandria. Mosby called him the "bogus Governor" because his authority was only in Union-controlled areas. The five raiders called at the City Hotel where Pierpont leased a suite, but the "Governor" had gone to Washington City that evening.

When Pierpont later learned that he had almost been captured, he was incensed, especially because of the note he received, supposedly from Mosby, stating, "You did not see the farmer who rode by your hotel on a hay wagon yesterday, did you Governor? My driver pointed out your window, and I marked it plain. It's just over the bay, and I'll get you some night, mighty easy."

Pierpont complained to Stanton, "This conduct on their part is impudent and Wicked and must be stopped or the whole Union sentiment within our lines will be demoralized." He did feel comforted that he kept his family in Pennsylvania and Maryland, safe from guerrillas.

The raiders rode south on Telegraph Road to Rose Hill, the home of Pierpont's aide, Colonel Daniel French Dulany, about four miles south of

Francis Pierpont is considered the "Father of West Virginia." Mosby referred to him as the "bogus governor" and attempted to capture him from Alexandria, Virginia. *Author's collection.*

Alexandria City. They had no problem finding the house because one of them was Private French Dulany, the colonel's son. The war was not only brother against brother; it was also father against son. As they entered, they found Colonel Dulany in bed. Young French greeted his surprised father, "How do Pa—I'm very glad to see you." Bolting upright in his bed, his father replied, "Well sir, I'm damned sorry to see you." Feeling sorry for his son, Colonel Dulany remarked that there was an old pair of shoes around the house that he had better take with him, "as he reckoned they were darned scarce in the Confederacy," whereupon the son, holding up his leg, which was encased in one of a pair of cavalry boots just captured from a sutler, asked the old man what he thought of that. A short distance away, they set fire to the railroad bridge over Cameron Run, which was quickly extinguished without much damage.

It is interesting what Mosby was writing to his wife at this time:

Fauquier Co.
October 1st, 63
My dearest Pauline
I am now at Mr. Ashby's—just returned from a raid. I went down in the suburbs of Alexandria and burned a railroad bridge within a quarter of a mile of two forts and directly in range of their batteries. Also captured Col. Dulaney, Aide to Pierpont. Dulaney lives in Alexandria, has a son in my command who was with me at the time. I have also made another [raid] as you see from my report enclosed. I send you some slips from Yankee papers. On my return I was most enthusiastically received. I stopped a few moments at Mr. Hathaway's yesterday. … It was quite an amazing scene, the interview between Dulaney and his son. Just as we were about to leave the Colonel sarcastically remarked to his son that he had an old pair of shoes he had better take as he reckoned they were d—d scarce in the Confederacy. Whereupon the son, holding up one leg which was encased in a fine pair of cavalry boots just captured from a sutler, asked the old man what he thought of that. I am now fixing my trigger for several good things which if they succeed will make a noise. Old Mrs. Shacklett is going to Baltimore next week and I shall send for some things for you all. By the by I forgot to tell you about my namesake. On my last trip I stopped at the house of a Mrs. Ferguson. She asked me if I didn't want to see "Mosby." Told her yes and she brought out a boy several months old who, she said, was named Mosby Ashby Jackson. Down near Alexandria I rode up to the house of an Irishman. Discovering who I was he went in, told his wife, who came running with a baby in her arms she said was named "Mosby." She had one two-year-old named Stonewall Jackson. In Richmond I got some torpedoes [mines] and my next trip I shall try to blow up a railroad train. I went to see the Secretary of War. He spoke in the highest terms of the services my command had rendered, said he read all of my official reports. Also saw old General Lee. He was very kind to me and expressed the greatest satisfaction at the conduct of my command. Kiss the children for me. My love to all.

> *Your affectionately,*
> *Jno. S. Mosby*

The horses that Aaron carried over I want sold. You can take the money. Perhaps you best invest it in tobacco. They ought to bring $2,000.

Mosby could report to Lee that with eight men, he had succeeded in disrupting the Union's rear guard communications and capture a Yankee colonel. Stuart wrote on the report that Mosby was "faithfully carrying out" his instructions, and Lee gave him great credit for "boldness and skill." The *New York Herald* reported Dulany's capture with the complaint, "Guerillas seem to be as plentiful in Fairfax County as our own troops and more active. Until a regiment is stationed at Fairfax Court House and another at Vienna, we may anticipate the continued and frequent depredations of these bands."

In menacing Meade's rear with thirty men, Mosby had embarrassed the enemy by seizing unguarded wagons in broad daylight and captured the aide of the "bogus" governor just a few miles from Washington City. He had forced Union cavalry to convoy sutler wagons with a strong escort. True to classic guerrilla tactics, he remained flexible on missions, concentrated on enemy weaknesses and preserved his command for further service. He had learned the valuable lesson that to satisfy Lee he must continue making scouting reports and give future raids and official reports a strong tone of contribution to the main army effort.

When Meade's army moved to Centreville to counter Lee's advance during the Bristoe Station Campaign of October 1863, Stuart sent out Mosby to scout in Meade's rear between Centreville and Washington City. The battalion increased to two companies as of October 1, but Mosby only had about fifty men. On October 17, Mosby concealed them in woods near Frying Pan and after dark went with seven men to Chantilly, about three miles north of Meade's headquarters. They were hiding in the pines along Little River Turnpike when an unescorted wagon train came into view. They let it pass and fell in behind, pretending to be a rear guard. Passing through an army camp, they saw enemy infantry on each side of the pike, cooking their suppers. The sky was cloudy, and no one suspected that the cavalry "escort" wore gray. Beyond the last picket post, Mosby gave a signal and the raiders drew their revolvers and surrounded the wagons, forcing the drivers to unhitch. They captured thirteen prisoners, seven horses and thirty-six mules. This was one of Mosby's many wagon raids.

During the six days that Meade's army was at Centreville, Mosby captured between seventy-five and one hundred prisoners and more than one hundred horses and mules. On October 19, the day that the Union army was moving toward Warrenton, Mosby sent two scouting reports indicating that the enemy was moving southwest from Fairfax Court House and Centreville. On October 20, Stuart forwarded the intelligence to Lee, once again demonstrating Mosby's importance as a useful set of eyes behind enemy lines. The Army of the Potomac had barely settled into camp near Warrenton when, on the night of October 26, Mosby's men

William Chapman, one of Mosby's leading lieutenants. By the end of the war, Chapman was second in command. *Author's collection.*

pretended to be Union soldiers in the middle of the army, only two miles from Meade's headquarters.

Using prior reconnaissance, intimate knowledge of the area and the cover of darkness, they reached a secluded stretch of the Warrenton-Gainesville Turnpike with trees on each side. Before long, a wagon train of about forty wagons appeared, guarded by Union cavalry, infantry and artillery in front and behind but with the center exposed. Thus the challenge was to stop the wagons in the center, unhitch the teams, set fire to the wagons and disappear before the escort could be alerted. Mosby directed Captain William Chapman to take ten men and stop the Union column by pretending to be Union cavalry.

William had been with Mosby over seven months, about the same time as his older brother, Sam, and both had fought at Miskel's Farm. Up to this point, William had been in Sam's shadow, for Sam was a Baptist minister and more outspoken. He sang hymns in a loud voice and loved fighting almost as much as Mosby. He fought so fiercely at Miskel's Farm that the enemy thought he was Mosby. Mosby liked Sam and appointed him adjutant, but he lacked William's gift of discretion, the ability to judge when an enemy could be attacked and defeated. Now Mosby was risking his expedition on William's ability to portray a Union provost marshal. William rode alongside a wagon and found out who was in charge of the artillery reserve, a lieutenant. Then he rode forward, found the lieutenant and arrested him under orders from headquarters, identifying himself as a captain of the Eighteenth Pennsylvania Cavalry on provost marshal duty. He ordered the teamsters to park along the road and unhitch their mules. At that point, Mosby and the other Rangers came out and joined in the roundup. Suddenly, a Union cavalry attachment appeared, and there was no time to fire the wagons; the raiders left in haste. They had captured 103 mules, 42 horses and about 30 prisoners without firing a shot.

Army gossip reported that Mosby had made off with four hundred mules, and a *New York Herald* correspondent at Meade's headquarters wrote, "Despite the precaution of strong pickets, the inevitable and inscrutable Mosby manages to break through our lines occasionally." Mosby divided the horses among his men and had the mules delivered to Stuart. At $110 in Union greenbacks, the drove of mules was worth over $11,000. When Stuart saw them, he said, "Hurrah for Mosby! This is a good haul. Mules! And fat, too!" He forwarded Mosby's report to the War Department with the endorsement, "This is but another instance of Major Mosby's skill and daring, in addition to those forwarded almost daily." And Seddon wrote, "Noted, with admiration at the fearlessness and skill of the gallant partisan." Within the month, William Chapman was unofficially commanding a separate company of Mosby's men and within two months, on December 15, was elected commander of new Company C.

On November 22, Mosby reported that the O&A Railroad was so well defended, with sentinels on the tracks in sight of each other and guards on all the trains, that he found it very difficult to attack. Three days later, Stuart approved, "Major Mosby is ever vigilant, ever active. The importance of his operations is shown by the heavy guard the enemy is obliged to keep to guard the railroad from his attacks." When the Union army left on the Mine Run Campaign on November 26, Meade left General John R. Kenly's division from the I Corps on duty as railroad guards, along with five hundred men of General David M. Gregg's cavalry division. Mosby, however, did not deserve full credit for this vigilance; Frank Stringfellow, a Stuart scout, and James C. Kincheloe of the Prince William County Partisan Rangers were active as well.

The problem with guarding the railroad was that the two Union commands did not connect. Devin's men were camped about two miles northeast of Culpeper, ten miles from where Kenly's line ended. They were ordered to guard the twelve miles from Culpeper to the linking point with Kenly at Rappahannock Station. About midway was Brandy Station, but since Meade had abandoned it as his supply center, Devin's cavalry did not patrol it the first night; there was a gap of five or six miles between Devin's and Kenly's men. By sundown on November 26, Mosby noticed the Union army move and found the gap on the O&A. With 125 Rangers—his most thus far—he proceeded to the northern bank of the Rappahannock River in the afternoon, concealed his men and scouted with three men. Late in the afternoon, they reached Brandy Station and saw a large wagon train escorted by a few infantry. Relying on audacity to mask the color of their uniforms in the fading light, Mosby and his men rode into their midst. He talked with the teamsters and the guards, determining that the wagons were lightly guarded. As Mosby's men started unhitching the mules, suddenly a sentinel fired a shot and all was bedlam as guns fired from all directions and mules and drivers ran in circles. The raiders burned between thirty and forty wagons, making off with 112 mules, seven horses and twenty prisoners.

Meade's turning movement failed, and his army returned north of the Rapidan River, going into winter quarters. By the end of the year, winter had come in with a vengeance, with temperatures hovering around zero. While the Union army huddled in their camps, Mosby was plotting new adventures for the New Year.

CHAPTER 5

A Thorn in the Side of the Yankees

1864

On January 1, 1864, eighty members of Colonel Henry A. Cole's Maryland Cavalry, led by Captain A.N. Hunter, entered the region of Mosby's Confederacy around Upperville and Rectortown. With Mosby off on a scout in Fairfax County, Ranger Captain William Smith rounded up thirty-two men and set off in pursuit of the Federals. The Rangers caught up with Hunter's force near Middleburg. Hunter quickly deployed his men into battle line just as Smith ordered a charge. The Federal line soon crumbled when Hunter's horse was killed, tumbling the captain to the ground. The Union cavalry hastily retreated toward Middleburg, but not before losing fifty-seven killed, wounded or captured, as well as sixty horses seized by the Rangers.

Cole's cavalry was one of two Union cavalry units organized along the border of Northern Virginia and given authority by Secretary of War Edwin M. Stanton to conduct independent operations. The other was one of the most persistent and long-standing opponents of Mosby's men, the Loudoun Rangers. Cole recruited his men from Maryland, Pennsylvania and the Unionist area of northern Loudoun County. Like the Loudoun Rangers, they had the disadvantage of conducting independent warfare surrounded by hostile civilians once they left Maryland or northern Loudoun. As they were local rivals, Mosby and his men sometimes underestimated both units.

Within a week, Cole's camp atop Loudoun Heights had been discovered, thanks to the work of Frank Stringfellow, staff officer and spy under Stuart temporarily attached to Mosby's command. Angered by the audacity of

Cole's cavalry to raid so deep into Mosby's territory and encouraged by the enemy's woeful performance at Middleburg, Mosby decided to attack Cole's main force, hoping to catch them unaware in their camp.

On January 9, Mosby ordered a rendezvous at Upperville, to which one hundred Rangers responded. The partisan company set out for Loudoun Heights through deep snow and bitter cold, reaching Woodgrove around 8:00 p.m. and stopping for two hours at the home of Ranger Henry Heaton. Just north of Hillsboro, they met up with Stringfellow and his scouting party, who informed Mosby of the exact location and strength of Cole's camp. Spotting Federal pickets along the Hillsboro Road, the Confederates headed east toward the wooded western slope of Short Hill Mountain, which they followed until they came to the bank of the Potomac River. From there they made their way along the riverbank to the base of Loudoun Heights. As the Rangers went up the mountain, they were forced to dismount, given the steep grade. They stopped within two hundred yards of the Union camp. Mosby sent a detachment under Stringfellow to capture Cole's headquarters in the rear of the camp, while he took the rest farther up the hillside, until they were directly west of the camp.

At around 3:00 a.m., as Mosby prepared to order the attack, gunfire erupted from the direction of Stringfellow's position, followed by the distant appearance of horsemen riding toward Mosby from the direction of the enemy camp. Thinking the unknown party consisted of Federals who had discovered Stringfellow and his men, Mosby ordered a charge. His Rangers descended on the camp and attacked the horsemen, who turned out to be Stringfellow's squadron. It was several minutes before the two parties recognized each other in the darkness, but not before several Confederates had been hit by friendly fire.

In the meantime, Cole's men were awakened by the gunfire. Led by Captain George Vernon, the men grabbed their weapons and hastily formed a dismounted battle line, though many were barely dressed. Despite the darkness, the Federals easily identified the Rangers, who stood out as they were the only ones on horses. Their initial volley dropped several Confederates, many of whom were caught out in the open along the road.

In the confusion of the forty-five-minute fight that followed, several Rangers retreated and, soon afterward, with the sound of Federal infantry approaching from Harpers Ferry, Mosby ordered a general withdrawal. The Rangers escaped with six prisoners (pickets from Company B of Cole's cavalry, all taken from along the Hillsboro Road) and nearly sixty horses but were forced to leave their dead and seriously wounded behind. A few miles

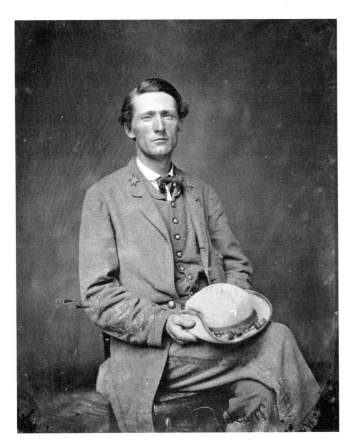

Mosby in his major's uniform, the rank he held for most of 1863. One star on the collar signified major; two stars, lieutenant colonel; and three stars, colonel. Laurel leaves around the stars signified brigadier general and higher. *Courtesy of the Library of Congress.*

beyond the Union camp, Mosby halted and sent two Rangers back under a flag of truce to exchange the prisoners for their dead and wounded, which included Captain Smith and First Lieutenant Thomas Turner. The Rangers left and made their way back toward Mosby's Confederacy.

Mosby's Rangers suffered fourteen casualties—four dead, four mortally wounded, five slightly wounded and one captured. Among the wounded was William "Willie" Mosby, John's younger brother. Of the dead, it was believed that three were victims of friendly fire. Cole suffered six dead, fourteen wounded, and six captured. For their performance in the fight, Cole was promoted from major to colonel and Vernon from captain to lieutenant colonel. The "Gallant Repulse of Mosby's Guerrillas" made front-page news in the North; reporters emphasized that Mosby left his dead lying in the bloodstained snow in the camp and that his line of retreat was marked by drops of blood on the snow-covered road. Northern journalists elevated the size of Mosby's force to four hundred men and praised Cole for his vigilance. Halleck gave the soldiers "high praise for their gallantry in repelling this rebel assault." They received a thirty-day furlough, and the people of Frederick, Maryland, honored them with a parade and banquet.

Mosby's men regarded the fight as "a little Waterloo." But the defeat earned Mosby the highest praise that he ever received from Stuart. Endorsing Mosby's report, Stuart wrote, "His sleepless vigilance and unceasing activity have done the enemy great damage. He keeps a large force of the enemy's cavalry continually employed in Fairfax in the vain effort to suppress his inroads. His exploits are not surpassed in daring and enterprise by those of petite guerre in any age. Unswerving devotion to duty, self-abnegation, and unflinching courage, with a quick perception and appreciation of the opportunity, are the characteristics of this officer."

He recommended Mosby's promotion to lieutenant colonel, which was officially approved effective January 21, only eleven days later. Seldom has a defeated commander received promotion and such praise for a setback.

Mosby was fortunate for his successes. In Richmond, Seddon had decided on November 26, 1863, to close the Partisan Ranger program, except for Mosby's and McNeill's Rangers. McNeill's Rangers were also commissioned under the Partisan Ranger Act. The 210-man battalion-size unit was formed from Company E of the Eighteenth Virginia Cavalry and the First Virginia Partisan Rangers (Sixty-second Virginia Mounted Infantry). John Hanson McNeill's forces operated in what became West Virginia. McNeill's Rangers were known to exercise military discipline when conducting raids. However, many Union generals considered McNeill and his men "bushwhackers," just as they felt about Mosby and his Rangers, not entitled to protection when captured, as was the case with other prisoners of war.

Captain McNeill's frequent raids on the towns of Piedmont, West Virginia, and Cumberland, Maryland, were aimed at disrupting the B&O Railroad service. It is estimated that over twenty-five thousand troops were diverted by Federal commanders to guard the B&O against McNeill's force. Piedmont, a small town at the foot of the Allegheny Mountains, was a frequent target due to its important machine shops and vast stores of railroad supplies.

After earlier raids were unsuccessful, McNeill finally succeeded in severing the railroad and burning the machine shops at Piedmont. This occurred in May 1864. The president of the B&O, John W. Garrett, reported to Stanton that "the extensive machine and carpenter shops of Piedmont have been burned. The engine and cars of the east-bound main train and two-tonnage trains have also been destroyed. Five other engines damaged…The heat of

McNeill's Raid into Maryland started in West Virginia. By the end of 1864, all Partisan Ranger activity in the Confederacy was outlawed, except for McNeill and Mosby. *Author's collection.*

the fire at the wreck of the trains at Bloomington had been too intense to permit much work, but during the night we expect to have the entire road again clear and train running regularly."

McNeill's official report to Seddon read, "We burned some seven large buildings filled with the finest machinery, engines, and railroad cars; burned nine railroad engines, some seventy-five or eighty burthern cars, two trains of cars heavily laden with commissary stores, and sent six engines with full head of steam toward New Creek. Captured the mail and mail train and 104 prisoners on the train."

A raid on a federal company guarding the bridge near Mount Jackson, Virginia, on October 3, was McNeill's last. In this foray, he was mortally wounded. He lingered on, suffering severe pain, until November 10. Ironically enough, John Hanson McNeill died in the same manner as his hero, Stonewall Jackson: he was shot accidentally by one of his own men.

McNeill's Rangers' greatest exploit happened in the last winter of the War. On February 22, 1865, John's son, Captain Jesse McNeill, and sixty-five raiders traveled sixty miles behind enemy lines to Cumberland. Without being detected, they captured both Union major general George Crook and Brigadier General Benjamin Kelley from their beds. They evaded pursuing Federal cavalry and delivered the captured generals to Lieutenant General Jubal A. Early, who forwarded the prisoners to Richmond.

On Christmas Day 1863, Seddon received a letter from Governor Zebulon V. Vance of North Carolina complaining that partisans were illegally seizing property and "committing depredations more outrageous than the plagues of Egypt." In January 1864, Seddon received a letter from General Thomas L. Rosser, commander of the Laurel Brigade, fighting the Yankees in the Shenandoah Valley. His experiences were with the partisan leaders John McNeill and Lieutenant Colonel Elijah "Lige" White. Lige had recruited his men from Loudoun County and Maryland for a border war but mustered them into the regular cavalry. He was an aggressive fighter, charging with sabers and revolvers, but his men fought informally like Indians, so Rosser called them "Comanches." Rosser believed the partisan corps was an evil nuisance that should be closed down. It kept men out of the regular ranks, lowered the morale of the regulars who were jealous and caused desertions.

Rosser wrote that he respected the gallant Mosby but turned one of Mosby's accomplishments on its head by stating that Mosby's men were of inestimable service to the Yankee army in keeping their men from straggling. Stuart endorsed his letter on January 18, agreeing that partisans were generally detrimental and pointing out that Mosby was the only efficient partisan that he knew and even Mosby usually operated with only one-fourth of his strength. Now Mosby had operated for one year, and still Stuart did not recognize that there was safety in dividing into small squads for raids. By sanctioning Rosser's recommendation, he was threatening Mosby's operations.

Lee agreed with Rosser and Stuart, stating, "As far as my knowledge and experience extends, there is much truth in the statement of General Rosser. I recommend that the law authorizing these partisan corps be abolished. The evils resulting from their organization more than counterbalance the good they accomplish."

Lee's solution was to do away with spoils reimbursement and bring worthy partisans such as McNeill and Mosby into the regular service for assignment on detached duty. Lee meant to make a temporary exception in Mosby's case, and he was not at all meaning to criticize Mosby. The day before, Lee had written a letter with one topic—the promotion of Mosby to lieutenant colonel in the Partisan Corps to "encourage him to still greater activity and zeal." He wanted Mosby to follow the example of fellow Virginian John D. Imboden, who organized the First Virginia Partisan Rangers, brought them into the regular forces and continued on duty in the Shenandoah Valley. Lee hoped that Mosby would at least increase to a regiment so that he could promote him to colonel.

But Mosby's mentors, Stuart and Lee, in attempting to reward and honor him, were threatening to shut him down because if he lost the reimbursement system he would not be able to raid successfully. Seddon used the letter as support for his bill of repeal. But he did give himself the authority to make exceptions—he was not going to allow Mosby and McNeill to be brought in. The bill passed the Confederate Congress on February 14, with his exemption provision intact. On April 1, Lee began a reorganization of the army by recommending that all partisans be disbanded immediately, except for Mosby. Lee wrote, "I am making an effort to have Colonel Mosby's battalion mustered into the regular service. If this cannot be done I recommend that the battalion be retained as partisans for the present."

Once again he commended Mosby for excellent service, enforcing discipline and protecting civilians.

Seddon received and approved Lee's letter on April 21, except for retaining Mosby's and McNeill's commands as raiders. Mosby himself did not learn of Rosser's letter until after the war, when he read it in the Confederate archives in Washington City. He responded, "There was scarcely a day that our command did not kill & capture more Yankees than Rosser did the whole time he was in the Valley."

As winter progressed in Northern Virginia, Mosby was as active as usual. On February 20, a detachment of Cole's Maryland Cavalry, two hundred strong, left Harpers Ferry for Upperville, where they surprised and captured eleven of the Rangers. They then set out south for Piedmont Station (present-day Delaplane), where shortly thereafter they came upon another partisan, Bill McCobb, who rushed to his horse but was thrown from it and killed when it jumped a fence.

Mosby, who was at the Heartland Farm on the road to Piedmont Station with four of his officers, was alerted of the oncoming Federals by a scout as they ate breakfast. The five Rangers rushed from the house to find the Federals on the road and immediately fired on the force. The unexpected gunfire surprised Cole, who withdrew his force back toward Upperville. The gunfire also roused sixty or so Rangers staying in the area. At Piedmont Station, the Rangers rendezvoused and set out in pursuit of the Federals, catching up with them at Upperville. A running fight ensued for three miles until Cole reached the ground of Blakley's Grove School and halted. There, he deployed his men behind a stone wall to contest the Rangers advance.

Mosby's men halted at the other side of the field, and a firefight broke out between the two lines.

Shortly thereafter, Cole ordered a charge. The Rangers repulsed the charge and counterattacked. Twice more the Federals charged as the fight swirled around the school, and twice more they were repulsed. Mosby then split his force in two and flanked Cole, forcing him to retire. As he withdrew, he placed skirmishers behind the numerous stone walls he crossed, impeding the Rangers' pursuit. In the fight, the Rangers killed six and wounded seven, while suffering only three wounded in addition to the eleven captured who were not liberated in the fight.

The following morning, 160 Rangers gathered to bury McCobb. At the same time, Major Charles Russell Lowell (his uncle was the poet James Russell Lowell) dispatched 167 troopers of the Second Massachusetts Cavalry and Sixteenth New York Cavalry under Captain James Sewall Reed on a raid into Loudoun County. At the funeral near Middleburg, Mosby learned of the Federal raid and mounted the Rangers in pursuit, sending the bulk of the force under William Chapman to Ball's Mill, south of Leesburg, while he and a small party shadowed the Federals. At Leesburg, Reed, not finding any sign of Confederates, set out east on the Leesburg Pike, camping six miles east of the town that night. As the Federals bivouacked, Mosby rejoined his main body, which he had since directed to Guilford Station (present-day Sterling) on the Alexandria, Loudoun and Hampshire Railroad. Upon rejoining the Rangers, Mosby led them to the pike, two miles west of Dranesville, and deployed them in three wings: a dismounted squad on the pike and two companies on each flank concealed in the woods to the sides of the road. A skirmish party was sent west on the pike as bait for the ambush.

At 10:00 a.m., the Federals broke camp and came upon Mosby's skirmishers an hour later. As the Federal vanguard in pursuit of the fleeing skirmishers came into sight, the flank wings sprung the trap, missing the main Federal force. Reed took advantage of the mistake and ordered a counterattack. The two forces collided in heavy hand-to-hand combat. At one point in the fighting, Ranger John Munson captured a Federal trooper but failed to take his side arm, and when he turned to rejoin the fight, the Yankee shot him in the back. Moments later, Ranger Baron Robert von Massow (a Prussian military officer) captured Reed, but he too failed to take his side arm and was also shot in the back. William Chapman wasted no time in killing Reed in retaliation. With Reed dead, the Federal resistance gave way, and the Rangers chased them north toward the Potomac River. Several of the Federal troopers jumped into the river in their haste to flee and drowned.

In the action, known to the Rangers as Second Dranesville, the Rangers killed twelve, wounded twenty-five and captured seventy, along with one hundred horses, while losing only five wounded and one killed.

By April 28, as spring was spreading in Northern Virginia, Lee was still at Orange Court House, trying to figure out what the new Northern commander, Ulysses Simpson Grant, would do in a spring campaign. On April 29, Lee informed President Davis that a scout in Washington City—not Mosby—had reported that a 23,000-man army under General Ambrose Burnside had moved from Annapolis to Alexandria on April 25. But Lee was not sure whether that army would march from Alexandria to the Rapidan River frontier from the north or take boats to threaten Richmond from the south.

Then at 1:45 p.m. on April 30, Mosby came through in his usual dramatic fashion. Mosby sent Lee a message that Burnside's force was passing through Centreville on April 28. Lee immediately telegraphed Davis renewing his request for reinforcements. He sent a letter that stated, "Lt. Col. Mosby, who was within a mile of Centreville on the 28th, the day that Burnside passed through, learned from prisoners that no troops were left in Annapolis except convalescents." Mosby's eyewitness report showed that Burnside was joining Meade, and a major offensive would jump off from the Rapidan. When Mosby wrote his summary report, Lee endorsed it, saying, "The services rendered by Colonel Mosby and his command in watching and reporting the enemy's movements have also been of great value."

Lee had to finally concede that Mosby's vision of his command, with separate small raiding forces attacking at different places simultaneously and commanded by Mosby clones, was effective. He congratulated Mosby for successfully multiplying himself. After his loss of Smith and Turner, Mosby still had William Chapman, and by April 29, when Union general Franz Sigel's offensive began in the Valley, Mosby had three additional replicas serving as officers in the battalion, now increased to four companies and over two hundred men. The new clones were young, handsome, intelligent and proficient in fooling the enemy, organizing an ambush and sensing whether a fight would succeed. Adolphus "Dolly" Richards was so much like Mosby that enemy commanders deceived and surprised by him often reported that he was Mosby. He was from Loudoun County, near Upperville, and had fought under Turner Ashby and, like Mosby, had served on the staff of Grumble Jones. Mosby made him captain at the age of nineteen and major at twenty.

Richard P. Montjoy, a Mississippi native who entered Confederate service in the Louisiana Infantry, rode the finest horses and dressed as

Richard Montjoy. Mosby considered him one of his best officers. *Author's collection.*

fastidiously as the men he commanded in Company D, Mosby's company of "dandies"—Marylanders who dressed in elaborate uniforms. He was killed in action in November at twenty-two years of age, racing his horse on a farm lane in Loudoun County in pursuit of four fleeing Union cavalrymen. As he came close, one of the Federals turned and fired his revolver, hitting Montjoy in the brain. Mosby issued a Special Order memorializing him as "an immortal example of daring and valor," and after the war, the men raised a monument over his grave in Warrenton. Alfred Glascock of Fauquier County, another veteran of Ashby's cavalry, once said to his men, "Now, boys, I am going to show you how to capture Yankees in the regular Mosby style," and with fourteen men captured twenty-nine. He succeeded Montjoy in command of Company D.

By this time in the war, Mosby and his men were achieving his goal of producing fear in the minds of the enemy as a force multiplier. Carl von Clausewitz, Prussian military theorist, in his book *On War*, stated that local bands of guerrillas should surround the invading army with a feeling of uneasiness and dread. Cuban communist guerrilla leader Che Guevera taught that invaders should be made to feel, day and night, that everything

80

outside of camp is hostile, that they are "inside hostile jaws." Mao Tse Tung identified the enemy's mind as the target and proposed that it was more important to attack his will than his body. Guerrillas should, he declared, cause the invader "constant mental worry," with harassment as irritating as a swarm of "innumerable gnats." William Cullen Bryant, in his poem *Song of Marion's Men*, mentioned the fear created in the minds of the British invaders by Mosby's hero of the American Revolution, Francis Marion:

> *And they who fly in terror deem*
> *A mighty host behind,*
> *And hear the tramp of thousands*
> *Upon the hollow wind*

Union cavalry on duty against Mosby on the Washington City cavalry screen felt surrounded even though they far outnumbered his small force. "Bands of guerrillas like so many ravenous beasts and birds of prey, hover around our lines, attacking wherever an opportunity offers plunder," one wrote in May 1863. Colonel Henry S. Ganesvoort wrote his father on October 1, 1863: "In fact, the whole country, in our rear, front, and flanks, is full of guerrillas," and in July 1864: "He is continually around us." A trooper informed the *Baltimore American*, "In fact, we are surrounded by guerrillas."

Toward night, when the shadows of the trees lengthened and the dark deepened in the forest, one imagined lurking danger so that riding between patches of woods close on each side of the road was a gauntlet of fear. One night in the winter of 1863–64, about 150 men of the First Rhode Island Cavalry scouted for Mosby south of the Rappahannock River. They were veterans, and the expedition was unremarkable until their return to camp about 11:00 p.m. The night was cold and clear, and as they approached a wooded area, they heard hoof beats pounding on the frozen road. They drew their sabers and charged, capturing two African Americans on two poor mules. The regimental historian wrote, "The spectre of Mosby and his gang had vanished."

It was a mistake to stay overnight inside Mosby's Confederacy unless the detachment had a strong commander and a contingent of infantry to provide a feeling of security, for the night belonged to Mosby and his men. Rangers would roll wagons toward the Union camps and shout commands to imaginary artillery and infantry and, when everything seemed prepared, yell, "Are you ready to surrender now Yankees?" They attempted to lure men into ambush by sending a civilian into the camp with word that Mosby

Herman Melville, author of *Moby Dick*. In order to get a taste of war, he rode with Union cavalry in April 1864. In his 114-verse epic poem, *The Raid Toward Aldie*, he compares Mosby to a shark gliding through green dark. *Courtesy of the Library of Congress.*

himself was present and this was their chance to capture him. They would keep the Federals awake by firing revolvers and lighting fireworks, and when it was time for changing of the guard, a few Rangers pretending to be Union soldiers would march up to a picket and announce with authority, "Corporal of the guard with third relief," and take the man captive. "How we longed for daylight!" one man exclaimed. "Drenched with rain, half-frozen, not daring to make a fire, having nothing to eat but dry hardtack, and not even cold water to wash it down, we were miserable, indeed."

The fear and feelings of Union cavalrymen were brought to life by Herman Melville, who went as a civilian observer on a raid led by Charles Russell Lowell, April 18–20, 1864. Melville was a friend of Lowell and a cousin of one of Lowell's regimental commanders, Henry Ganesvoort, Thirteenth New York Cavalry. Melville's career had fallen on hard times since his novel, *Moby Dick*, published in 1851, had been received with mixed reviews. Like many Americans, Melville recognized the deep significance of the Civil War and began writing war poems, such as "Balls Bluff: A Reverie" and "Stonewall Jackson: Mortally Wounded at Chancellorsville," hoping to become poet laureate of the Civil War. But he had no military experience and needed to have a first-hand taste of war. He was visiting Lowell's brigade headquarters on April 18 when Lowell started on a scout for Mosby and his men and invited Melville to ride along. This would be his only war experience.

As it turned out, Lowell was the most cautious yet successful opponent that Mosby faced on a continual basis. Lowell took about 500 men: 250 cavalry and 250 infantry. He had learned that it helped him to remain calm and kept his men from getting spooked. He knew that Mosby would not knowingly come near infantry. He sent his infantry to set up camp at Ball's Mill on Goose Creek, northeast of Aldie. He departed Vienna between 9:00 and 10:00 a.m. on April 18 with the cavalry detachment, including Melville, riding horseback in the column.

Joining the infantry at Ball's Mill at 4:00 p.m., they dismounted, fed the horses, ate supper and remounted at 5:00 p.m., crossed Goose Creek and headed toward Leesburg, where Mosby's men were reportedly foraging for corn. Lowell's troopers rode into Leesburg as they were fired upon from south of town. Pickets were sent out but with little rest as Mosby's men fired signal rockets from nearby hills. At daylight, after a cold breakfast with no fires, Lowell sent parties into the woods, where they surrounded a party of Mosby's men, capturing eleven and mortally wounding one. At 10:00 a.m., Lowell marched back to Goose Creek, and his cavalry were in camp protected by the infantry at 4:00 p.m. when a Unionist civilian reported that Mosby himself had just passed through fields about two miles away. Lowell and his men galloped to Aldie, where the citizens reported that Mosby had just been there and left a note of regard for Lowell. Since he now knew that Mosby was aware of his presence, he decided not to go toward Rectortown or Upperville.

Instead he decided to take advantage of civilian intelligence that some of Mosby's men were attending a wedding that evening in Leesburg. Lowell sent seventy-five cavalrymen dismounted; they arrived thirty minutes after the party had ended. The Union men lost one killed and three wounded in a firefight. Lowell had conformed to his conservative style and protected his men from ambush. His men had appeared three times in Leesburg where Mosby's men had been reported. Losing one killed and three wounded and mortally wounding one Rebel and capturing eleven, his mission could be called a success. As a result of his experience, Melville returned home and wrote "The Raid Toward Aldie," a 114-verse poem, included in his book of war poems, *Battle-Pieces and Aspects of the War*, of which the first and last stanzas follow:

> *The cavalry-camp lies on the slope*
> *Of what was late a vernal hill,*
> *But now like a pavement bare—*
> *An outpost in the perilous wilds*
> *Which ever are lone and still;*
> *But Mosby's men are there—*
> *Of Mosby best beware.*

> *Now halt the verse, and turn aside—*
> *The cypress falls athwart the way;*
> *No joy remains for bard to sing;*
> *And heaviest dole of all is this,*
> *That other hearts shall be as gay*
> *As hers that now no more shall spring:*
> *To Mosby-land the dirges cling.*

Every verse contains a reference to Mosby. Melville described the hostility of Mosby's civilian supporters to the Union men and mentioned that Mosby had no camp and used hit-and-run tactics. He emphasized that the Union goal was to capture Mosby himself, recognized the use of pro-Union civilian guides and intelligence from prisoners of war and noted the physical and mental exhaustion resulting from the scout.

Actually, fear took on a life of its own, and imagination multiplied Mosby's force far beyond its actual strength or presence. Mosby said that three hundred men skillfully led in the rear were equal to ten thousand on the fighting front, especially in terms of disruptions and false alarms. His small battalion was never a real threat to Washington City, but whenever a cloud of dust or plume of smoke would rise in the sky along the Potomac River, civilians in Maryland would go into a panic, and the commanders in Washington City would alert the pickets to take up the planks on the Chain Bridge to prevent Mosby's men from entering the capital. When Mosby was expected, soldiers would move artillery to the riverbank on the Washington City side: two mountain howitzers aimed across the deck of the bridge and two rifled six-pounders on a hill a few yards in the rear. At 9:00 p.m., the lieutenant in charge would have the planks removed.

On July 2, Mosby was informed of Lieutenant General Jubal A. Early's plans to invade Maryland by the latter's quartermaster, Hugh Swartz, who was then traveling through Fauquier County. In order to aid Early's raid, Mosby planned a raid into Maryland of his own to cut telegraph wires between Washington City and Harpers Ferry. Accordingly, he ordered a rendezvous of the Rangers the following morning at Rectortown, to which 250 Rangers responded. They spent the day in the saddle, making it to Purcellville by day's end, and made camp for the night. The next morning, July 4, the Rangers traveled the rest of the distance to the Potomac River, arriving across from Berlin (present-day Brunswick, Maryland) around 11:00 a.m., whereupon scouts were dispatched along the river to find possible targets of attack. When they returned, Mosby was informed of a small Union force at Point of Rocks, Maryland. Mosby determined this would be the Rangers' target.

That same day, one hundred troopers of the Second Massachusetts Cavalry and fifty from the Thirteenth New York Cavalry under Major William H. Forbes were dispatched from Falls Church into Loudoun County by Lowell to hunt down Mosby and his Rangers. The force stopped at Ball's Mill on Goose Creek for the night.

Upon arriving across the river from Point of Rocks, the Rangers found the village held by two companies of Federal infantry and two companies of cavalry in the form of the Loudoun Rangers, totaling 350 Federals in all. One of the companies of infantry was stationed on Patton's Island in the middle of the Potomac, while the second occupied a small fort on high ground above the C&O Canal. The Loudoun Rangers were encamped in the village. Mosby immediately set to work clearing Patton's Island in preparation for crossing the river. He deployed Sam Chapman with his lone howitzer on the bluff above the riverbank and ordered a detachment of sharpshooters under Lieutenant Albert Wrenn to wade into the river and attack the Federal position on the island. The Federal infantry exchanged fire with the Rangers for several minutes before giving way to the combined rifle and artillery fire and fled to the Maryland shore, tearing up the small bridge over the canal as they crossed it. The Rangers then dashed across the river to the Maryland shore, where they began exchanging fire with the Federals across the canal. Many of the Rangers immediately set about repairing the bridge using planking from an old building. As soon as it was complete, the Rangers ran across, led by Hatcher, who ran into the Union camp under heavy fire and captured its flag. Once across the canal, the Rangers quickly drove the Federals from the town.

With the Union garrison dispatched, the Rangers set about burning canal boats and cutting the telegraph wires that ran beside the river from Washington City to its garrison at Harpers Ferry. Besides Point of Rocks strategic value, it was also the refuge of many prominent Loudoun Unionists and their property, including the Loudoun Rangers' commander, Samuel C. Means. Thus after effecting the disruption of travel and communication along the Potomac, the Rangers set about pilfering the stores and warehouses of the town, some of which contained property of Loudoun Unionists. Because of the numerous pieces of fine clothing the Rangers returned with, the raid became known as the Calico Raid. After completing the raid, the Rangers retired back to Virginia and camped along the road to Leesburg.

The following morning, Mosby dispatched about one hundred Rangers to escort three wagons full of plunder back to Fauquier County. He also dispatched Rangers Fount Beattie and Harry Heaton to report to Early, who was camped near Antietam Creek, with the message that Mosby's command would coordinate with his. Mosby then led his Rangers back to Point of Rocks to continue his raid into Maryland. The actions of the Rangers, however, had not gone unnoticed in Washington City, and after learning of the raid, Halleck dispatched the Eighth Illinois Cavalry from Washington City to Point of Rocks. When the Rangers arrived at the banks of the Potomac, they found the Eighth Illinois holding the village. A ninety-minute firefight across the river ensued, in which the Eighth Illinois claimed to kill one and wound two Rangers while suffering no casualties themselves (Mosby made no record of any casualties) before Mosby broke off the attack and headed toward Leesburg. The Eighth Illinois was soon dispatched from Point of Rocks to Monocacy Junction, where Union major general Lew Wallace was assembling a ragtag force to oppose Early's drive on Washington City and, along with the Loudoun Rangers, would fight in the Battles of Frederick and the Monocacy.

As Mosby approached Leesburg, his scouts reported to him the presence of the Federals under Major Forbes in the town. In response, Mosby led the Rangers into camp west of Leesburg on Catoctin Mountain where they spent the night. The Federals departed from Leesburg the next morning, July 6, and headed south by Oatlands Mill and on to Aldie. At around 6:00 p.m., the Federals arrived at the intersection with the Little River Turnpike and stopped to rest for an hour or so at the Skinner farm near Mount Zion Church.

Mount Zion Church today. One of Mosby's greatest victories happened here on July 6, 1864. *Author's collection.*

Meanwhile, Mosby entered Leesburg shortly after the Federals left and learned of their withdrawal. He led the Rangers out of town toward Ball's Mill on the Old Carolina Road, believing that the Federals had returned on the same route they had arrived on. At Ball's Mill, Mosby was informed by local citizens of his mistake, whereupon he devised a plan to head southeasterly toward Gum Springs (present-day Arcola) and intercept the Federals as they traveled east on the Little River Turnpike.

Upon arriving at Gum Springs, Mosby deployed his scouts, who located the Federal force a half mile away on the western slope of a small ridge that lay between the two forces. Mosby deployed his howitzer on the crest of the ridge and formed his command on the turnpike in columns of four led by Hatcher with a dozen skirmishers in advance. The skirmishers encountered Forbes's pickets just as the Federals were preparing to leave. Alerted by his pickets, Forbes quickly assembled his men into two lines in a field south of the pike and prepared to charge the oncoming Rangers. The shots of the skirmishers also alerted Sam Chapman manning the howitzer that let out a shot, which, though not well aimed, caused disruption in the Federal line. Seeing that he could no longer order a charge, Forbes attempted to redeploy his lines to meet a charge. The disruption gave the Rangers time to dismantle a rail fence that stood between them and the Federals. Upon its removal, the Rangers charged, delivering a deadly volley at the re-forming Federal lines and startling the Federals' horses, sending their ranks into disarray.

The Federals broke southwest past the Skinner house and Mount Zion Church. For his part, Forbes attempted to rally his men, getting them to re-form a line in the woods southwest of the pike. In the woods, the two forces collided in fierce close-range fighting. The Federals drew their sabers but found them ineffective against the Rangers' pistol fire. In close-quarter fighting, Forbes encountered Mosby and attempted to stab him with his saber. Thomas Richards jumped in front of the blade, taking it in the shoulder and saving his commander. Mosby emptied his pistol, shooting out Forbes's horse from under him and throwing Forbes to the ground. He quickly surrendered, and the Federal resistance finally gave way. The Yankees broke into retreat with the Rangers in pursuit for several miles.

The hour-long fight, known as the Action at Mount Zion Church, proved to be one of the Rangers' most complete victories. They inflicted severe casualties, killing twelve, including Captain Goodwin Stone, wounding thirty-seven, taking fifty-seven prisoners, including Forbes, and capturing every horse not injured or killed in the fight, totaling 71 percent of the total Federal force present. The Rangers suffered one mortally wounded and six casualties. In addition, the telegraph wires that were cut at Point of Rocks during the Calico Raid would hinder the Federal pursuit of Early following the Battle of Fort Stevens.

Union commander Grant, reacting to the political commotion caused by Early's invasion, organized the Middle Military Division, whose field troops were known as the Army of the Shenandoah, led by Major General Philip Sheridan. By August, Sheridan launched a campaign to drive Confederate forces out of Virginia's Shenandoah Valley. Sheridan organized his army in the northern end of the Valley in the vicinity of Harper's Ferry. This was an area where Mosby and his Rangers had been carrying out successful raids and guerrilla operations against Union forces for a year and a half. Mosby may have had some resentment against Sheridan, for Sheridan's troopers had mortally wounded Jeb Stuart at Yellow Tavern, just north of Richmond, on May 11. Mosby immediately began attacking Sheridan's supply trains, cavalry detachments and other targets of opportunity. Federal forces spent considerable time and effort to stop the Rangers, and at one point, the conflict turned vicious beyond the normal parameters of war.

On September 23, Captain Samuel Chapman and a force of about 120 Rangers attacked a Union army wagon train near Front Royal. Chapman thought the wagon train had no cavalry escort and would be an easy target. But as he divided his men into two columns for the attack, a brigade of Regular Army cavalry under the command of Lowell appeared.

Chapman's force was in danger of being trapped or destroyed, and he ordered the two columns to withdraw as quickly as possible. But Lowell attacked before the Rangers could get away. The Federals nearly surrounded the Rangers, but the raiders were able to push their way out and escape. The Union cavalry pursued and took six prisoners before ending the chase.

Lieutenant Charles McMaster of the Second U.S. Cavalry was one of the Federal casualties, killed by a bullet to the head. Some of the Union cavalrymen thought McMaster had been killed after he had surrendered. When this report reached the Federals in Front Royal, the Union men were outraged. Lowell's command arrived at Front Royal with the six prisoners, and the Federals called for revenge for McMaster's death.

Besides Lowell, senior officers present included Brigadier Generals Wesley Merritt and George A. Custer. In retaliation for McMaster's death, the execution of the six Ranger prisoners was ordered. Though many, including Mosby himself, would blame Custer for the executions, Lowell wrote that it was Merritt who gave the order. Years later, Mosby clarified his position. Custer and the other senior officers present made no attempt to stop the executions and went along with it, so in Mosby's view they shared responsibility for the incident. Also, some of Custer's men participated in the executions.

Three of the prisoners were taken out and shot. Another prisoner, seventeen-year-old Henry Rhodes, was not a member of the Rangers but wanted to be one. He had grabbed a horse and joined in the retreat of some of Mosby's men as they passed through Front Royal and was captured. Rhodes's mother begged for her son's life to no avail; in perhaps the most brutal event of the day, one of Custer's cavalrymen shot Rhodes to death in his mother's presence.

Two other prisoners were interrogated and promised their lives would be spared in exchange for information on Mosby, but they refused to talk. They were then executed by hanging. A sign was placed on one of the victims declaring, "Such is the fate of all of Mosby's men."

When Mosby himself heard about the executions, he was furious and determined to retaliate. He proposed to General Lee that he would execute an equal number of Custer's men for those Rangers executed by the Federals. Lee and Seddon approved the proposal.

The site of the execution of Mosby's Rangers by Union soldiers in Front Royal, Virginia, in September 1864. *Author's collection.*

On November 6 at Rectortown, twenty-six recently captured prisoners from Custer's command were informed that they were to draw lots to select seven men for execution (a seventh Ranger had been executed in a separate incident). Six men and a drummer boy made the unlucky draws; a second drawing was held to spare the drummer boy.

The unfortunate seven were taken a few miles away to an area near Berryville, by a Ranger detachment under the command of Lieutenant Ed Thomson. Three of the seven were hanged, and two were shot. The two who were shot were wounded but not fatally. Two other prisoners managed to escape and made it back to Union lines. A note was left on one of the hanged men that stated, "These men have been hung in retaliation for an equal number of Colonel Mosby's men, hung by order of General Custer at Front Royal. Measure for measure."

Although only three Union prisoners had actually been executed, Mosby believed he had accomplished his purpose. Mosby wrote a letter to Sheridan explaining what had happened and his reasons for retaliating.

Nov. 11, 1864
Major General P.H. Sheridan
Commanding U.S. Forces in the Valley
General:
 Sometime in the month of September during my absence from my command, six of my men who had been captured by your forces were hung and shot in the streets of Front Royal by the order and in the immediate presence of Brigadier General Custer. A label was attached to the clothes of one of the murdered men declaring that "such would be the fate of Mosby and all his men." So far from either yourself or your government disclaiming this act of brutality they have lately rewarded the criminal [Custer] with a Major General's commission. Since the murder of my men not less than seven hundred prisoners including many officers of high rank captured from your army by my command have been forwarded to Richmond but the execution of my purpose of retaliation was deterred in order if possible to confine it if practicable to the men of Custer and Powell. On the 6th inst. seven of your men by my order were executed on your highway of travel, the Valley Pike. Hereafter any prisoners falling into my hands will be treated with kindness due to their condition unless some new act of barbarity shall compel me to reluctantly adopt a course at which humanity shudders.

Very respectfully,
Your obedient servant,
John S. Mosby, Lieutenant Colonel

There were no more executions by either side. After the war, Mosby summed up his reasoning for the retaliatory executions, saying, "It was not an act of revenge, but a judicial sentence to save not only the lives of my own men, but the lives of the enemy. It had that effect. I regret that fate thrust such a duty upon me; I do not regret that I faced and performed it."

As he operated in Sheridan's rear, the railroad that brought Sheridan his supplies was his weak point and consequently Mosby's favorite object of attack. For security it had to be closely guarded by detachments of troops, which materially reduced his offensive strength. Mosby kept watch for unguarded points, and the opportunity they offered was never lost.

Early in October, one of Mosby's best men, Jim Wiltshire, afterward a prominent physician in Baltimore, reported a gap through which the Rangers might penetrate between the guards and reach the B&O Railroad without exciting an alarm. It was a hazardous enterprise, as there were camps along

The site of the "Yankee Lottery" in Rectortown, Virginia. This was Mosby's response in November 1864 to what he considered the murder of his Rangers by Union soldiers. *Author's collection.*

the line and frequent communication between them, but it would injure Sheridan to destroy a train and compel him to place stronger guards on the road. So Mosby resolved to take the risk. Wiltshire had a timetable and knew the minute when the train was due and timed the attack so that it would not have to wait long.

The western-bound passenger train was selected from the schedule as it would create a greater sensation to burn it than any other; it was due about 2:00 a.m. on the morning of October 14, between Martinsburg and Harpers Ferry, West Virginia. Wiltshire led the men to a long, deep cut on the railroad. No patrol or picket was in sight. Mosby preferred derailing the train in a cut to running it off an embankment, because there would be less danger of the passengers being hurt.

It was a bright and clear night. Mosby was probably the only Raider who went through the war without a watch, but all of his men had watches and knew it would not be long before the train would be due. Videttes were sent out, and the men were ordered to lie down on the bank of the railroad and keep quiet. They had ridden all day, so they were soon peacefully asleep. They did not hear the train coming until it got up in the cut; Mosby and his men were aroused and astounded by an explosion and a crash. As a rail had been displaced, the engine had run off the track, the boiler burst and the air was filled with red-hot cinders and escaping steam. Above all could be heard the screams of the passengers—especially women. Knowing that the railroad guards would soon hear of it and that no time was to be lost, Mosby ran along the line and pushed his men down the bank, ordering them to go to work pulling out the passengers and setting fire to the cars.

Mosby stood on the bank giving directions to his men. One of them reported that a car was filled with Germans and that they would not get out. He told him, "Set fire to the car and burn the Dutch, if they won't come out." They were immigrants going west to locate homesteads and did not understand a word of English or what all this meant. They had through tickets and thought they had a right to keep their seats. There were a lot of copies of the *New York Herald* on the train for Sheridan's army. The men circulated the newspapers through the train and applied matches. Suddenly, the immigrants now took in the situation and came tumbling out of the flames.

A great many ludicrous incidents occurred. One lady ran up to Mosby and exclaimed, "Oh, my father is a Mason!" He had no time to say anything but "I can't help it." One passenger claimed immunity for himself on the grounds that he was a member of an aristocratic church in Baltimore.

Two of his men, Charlie Dear and West Aldridge, reported that they had two U.S. Army paymasters with their satchels of greenbacks. Knowing it would be safer to send them out by a small party, which could easily elude the enemy, one of the lieutenants, Charlie Grogan, was sent with two or three men to take them over the Blue Ridge to the rendezvous point.

The civilians, including the ladies, were left to keep warm by the burning cars, and the soldiers were taken as prisoners. Among the latter was a young German lieutenant who had just received a commission and was on his way to join his regiment in Sheridan's army. Mosby was attracted by his personal appearance, struck up a conversation with him and rode next to him for several miles. He was dressed in a fine beaver overcoat, high boots and a new hat with gilt cord and tassel. Mosby said to him, "We have done you no harm. Why did you come over here to fight us?" "Oh," he said, "I only come to learn de art of var." Mosby left him and rode to the head of the column, as the enemy was about, and there was a prospect of a fight. It was not long before the German came trotting up. There had been such a vast change that he was scarcely recognizable. One of the Rangers had exchanged his

Twenty-dollar U.S. greenback. Mosby and his men destroyed a train of the B&O Railroad in October 1864 near Harpers Ferry, West Virginia. He divided the captured $173,000 equally among his men who had taken part in the Greenback Raid. *Author's collection.*

old clothes with him for his new ones, and he complained about it. Mosby asked the German if he had not told him that he came to Virginia to learn the art of war.

"Yes," he replied.

"Very well," Mosby said, "this is your first lesson."

Before reaching the Shenandoah River, a citizen informed them that Captain Richard R. Blazer was roving around the neighborhood looking for them. He commanded a picked corps, armed with Spencer carbines—seven-shooters—that had been assigned by Sheridan to the special duty of looking for Mosby. The Rangers anger was up when they heard that "Old Blaze," as they called him, was about. They were eager for a fight in which they could win more laurels. It was not long before Blazer's campfires were seen, where he had spent the night. The men rushed into the camp, but Blazer was gone. He had left before daybreak. But this only postponed his fate for a few weeks.

On November 18 at Kabletown, West Virginia, Mosby was able to defeat Blazer's Scouts, inflicting forty-two casualties, almost half of the Union force. In January 1865, Blazer's Scouts were officially disbanded.

The Shenandoah and Blue Ridge were crossed before noon, and Grogan's party was found with the greenbacks waiting at Bloomfield in Loudoun County. The men were ordered to dismount and fall in line, and three were appointed—Charlie Hall, Montjoy and Beattie—to open the satchels and count the money in their presence. Mosby ordered it to be divided equally among them, with no distinction to be made between officers and men. Each man received about $2,000 of the $173,000 captured. Mosby took nothing.

The burning of this train in the midst of Sheridan's troops and the capture of his pay and paymasters created a great sensation. Of course, the railroad people thought that Sheridan had not given adequate protection to their road. Lee's dispatch shows what he thought of the importance of the blow.

> *Chaffin's Bluff,*
> *October 16th, 1864.*
>   *On the 14th instant Colonel Mosby struck the Baltimore and Ohio Railroad at Duffield's, destroyed U. S. military train consisting of locomotive and ten cars, securing twenty prisoners and fifteen horses. Amongst the prisoners are two paymasters with $168,000 in Government funds.*
>   *R.E. Lee, General.*
>   *Hon. James A. Seddon, Secretary of War.*

The paymasters and other prisoners were sent to Libby Prison, and one of them, Major David Ruggles, died there. They were unjustly charged of being in collusion with Mosby, but their capture was simply an ordinary incident of war. As the government held them responsible for the loss of the funds, they had to apply to Congress for relief. After the war, Major Edwin Moore came to see Mosby to get a certificate that he had captured the money. The certificate stated that the report to General Lee of $168,000 captured was based upon erroneous information and was sent off before he had received the report of the commissioners appointed to count and distribute the money. The sum captured was $173,000.

For the next several days, a flurry of telegrams and reports were flying back and forth between Harpers Ferry and Washington City. From Seward, at Martinsburg, to Stevenson, at Harper's Ferry: "Four scouts have just arrived and reported that they were attacked about eight miles this side of Winchester by a party of fifty guerrillas this afternoon. They all seem to be positive that they were attacked by Mosby's men and that Mosby with one foot bound up was with them."

Mosby was there and with one foot bound up. A few days before the attack on the train, his horse had been shot in a fight, and a Yankee cavalryman rode over him, stepping on his foot and bruising it, so that for some time he could wear only a sock and had to use a cane when he walked. He was in this condition when the train was attacked.

Stanton, writing from Washington, replied to Stevenson at Harper's Ferry on October 14, saying, "It is reported from Martinsburg that the railroad has been torn up and a paymaster and his funds captured. When and where did this occur and have any measures been taken for recapture?"

Stevenson responded to Stanton, "Just heard from captured train. The attacking party was part of Mosby's command. They removed a rail, causing train to be thrown off track, then robbed the passengers and burned train. The point of attack was about two miles east of Kearneysville, about 2.30 A.M. Paymasters Moore and Ruggles with their funds were captured and carried off...The cavalry sent out in pursuit of Mosby's guerrillas, who burned the train, have returned. Report they failed to overtake them."

At that time, there were a number of paymasters at Martinsburg on their way to pay off Sheridan's soldiers, and they were now in a state of blockade. One of them who was shut up there said in a dispatch, "I have my funds in the parlor of the United States Hotel here, guarded by a regiment. The express train was burned eight miles west of Harper's Ferry between 2 and 3 o'clock this A.M. Major Ruggles' clerk escaped and is now with me...General Seward, who is in command here, says he will use all his efforts to protect us and our money. I shall make no move till I can do so with safety."

The Rangers' operations that day were not confined to the Shenandoah Valley but extended east of the Blue Ridge to the vicinity of Washington City, where preparations were made to keep them south of the Potomac. Later in the same day that the train was captured, Captain William Chapman, with two companies, crossed the Potomac a few miles east and struck the canal and railroad in Maryland. The alarm caused by the burning of the train in the morning had not subsided before news came of a fresh attack on the road at another point, and troops were hurried from Baltimore and other places to meet it. But, of course, when the troops got there, the damage had been done and the men had gone.

This meant that the railroad had to be more strongly guarded if communication was to be kept up between the Shenandoah Valley,

Washington City and Baltimore. Troops were rushed from many points to guard the railroad and the canal. Mosby's object had then been accomplished.

After the Greenback Raid, two of his companies, under Richards and Montjoy, made a demonstration on Washington City to keep reinforcements from Sheridan. Union general John P. Slough was ordered to send five hundred infantry to Annandale from Alexandria, to drive off the Rangers, who were thought to be only one hundred men. On October 17, Union troops at Falls Church were warned not to be surprised. When Mosby's men drove in the Yankee pickets, Union cavalry in Alexandria was again sent out, and the Fifth Wisconsin moved rapidly to Annandale. On October 18, the Eighth Illinois was sent down from Rectortown through Centreville to find the Rangers. A Ranger detachment under Montjoy entered Falls Church and was taking horses from the stables when a Union man, Reverend J.D. Read, blew a horn to alert the nearby Union cavalry camp. Montjoy's men captured Read and an African American member of the home guard. Read was a well-known abolitionist, originally from New York, and had been warned by the Rangers. Both men were marched out to the pine woods near Vienna and shot. Read died immediately; the black man's ear was shot off, and he pretended to be dead. For years afterward, the children in the area would skip rope and sing:

> *Isn't any school*
> *Isn't any teacher*
> *Isn't any church*
> *Mosby shot the preacher!*

Leading another raid himself in the Shenandoah Valley on the morning of October 25, Mosby captured another general. He had almost four hundred men, the largest number he had worked with. He divided his men into small parties in order to hinder Sheridan's lines of communications. As he was checking out the turnpike north of Winchester, an ambulance wagon was racing north, escorted by ten Union cavalry. Onboard was General Alfred Napoleon Alexander Duffie, a dapper Frenchman whom Sheridan had relieved of command of a cavalry division and assigned to remount camp near Hagerstown, Maryland, where he was heading. Duffie had taken part in operations against Mosby, promising to capture and bring him back to Washington City. Duffie would have been safe if he had remained with his full complement of fifty cavalry, but he impatiently rode forward, far ahead of his escort. Mosby captured him and three enlisted men. Sheridan remarked that Duffie was taken "by his own stupidity."

The two main questions for Sheridan and other Union commanders were, "Where is Mosby, and how can we capture or stop him?" The most effective Mosby hunters developed friendships with Unionist civilians and used them as guides. Deserters from Mosby's command were also used; they knew the Rangers' safe houses. Union officers learned to distrust white adults and asked directions from children and African Americans. Captured Rangers were no help, saying nothing. Frankland refused to tell where Mosby was, even after his interrogators marched him around carrying a fence rail. John Puryear remained silent even when his captors put a rope around his neck and twice pretended to hang him.

Union commanders used "Jessie Scouts"—Union soldiers in Confederate uniform—to gather intelligence. Sheridan had a company of these Jessie Scouts, and the Union cavalry in Fairfax County had scouts in Rebel uniforms. False Confederates became so common that at one point Mosby issued membership cards so that genuine Rangers could identify each other. By the end of 1864, any stranger in a Confederate uniform was assumed to be a Union spy until proven genuine.

Special Forces today practice capturing important enemies by studying the subject's daily routine in a targeting process known as "Figure Eight." Since most people are creatures of habit, one studies when a target's day begins, where he goes and who he sees, looking for a pattern and the ideal opportunity to capture him. This would not have worked on Mosby because, except for rare occasions, his movements were varied and unpredictable. He told no one where he planned to spend the night, and he usually settled down only after dark, so that informers had no idea where he was. Sometimes he slept alone or with one or two of his men in woods or orchards or fence corners, sleeping on the ground with a buffalo robe as a cover, but usually he slept in someone's home. Lowell said, "Mosby is an old rat and has a great many holes."

Throughout the fall of 1864, Sheridan had initiated total war in the Shenandoah Valley. Grant had told Sheridan in August, "Give the enemy no rest. Do all the damage to railroads and crops you can. Carry off stock of all descriptions, and negroes, so as to prevent further planting. If the war is to last another year, we want the Shenandoah Valley to remain a barren waste."

Sheridan later claimed to have destroyed two thousand barns and seventy mills.

On November 28, he brought the fire to Mosby's Confederacy. On that day his cavalry came through Ashby's Gap with rations, forage, ammunition and plenty of matches, descending into Loudoun County. For the next four days, residents could follow the line of march by the great columns of black

General Phil Sheridan. He is remembered for "the Burning" in the Shenandoah Valley and Loudoun County as General William T. Sherman is remembered in Georgia. *Author's collection.*

smoke rising over the countryside. To this day, it is remembered locally as "the Burning." In Harpers Ferry, a Union soldier wrote, "I can see from the window now the reflection of the fire glowing on the horizon, showing how completely the work of devastation is being carried out."

The purpose was to destroy Mosby's economic support, just as the previous burning in the Shenandoah had deprived Confederates of supplies from the fertile valley farms. Grant had first ordered the Loudoun-Fauquier Counties burnings back on August 16 in reaction to the wagon raids. He had directed Sheridan to send in his cavalry to arrest all men under fifty and destroy or carry off all crops, livestock and slaves. Now there were orders to destroy all forage and subsistence and burn all barns and gristmills and their contents. They were to burn no dwellings.

The orders were to put the torch to both pro-Confederate and pro-Union farmers in Loudoun County. The aspect that struck at Mosby the hardest was the destruction of corn and the ability to produce corn. In 1863, the Lincoln administration had recognized the need to open limited trade in occupied territories to allow loyal citizens to purchase subsistence. The Treasury Department issued permits to merchants to sell to loyalists in Union-occupied sections of the Confederacy, a program that applied perfectly to Loudoun Unionists. Selected merchants were required to sell only to persons who took the loyalty oath, but many with stores in southern Maryland and Loudoun County illegally sold to Confederate sympathizers as well.

It was reported to Sheridan that illegal trade continued between Maryland and Loudoun. Therefore, on December 8, about ten days after the Burning Raid, he ordered all trade under the jurisdiction of Harpers Ferry closed, including the Treasury Department stores. Smuggling continued, but this order, coupled with a Union blockade of the Potomac River, made the last four months of the war the most difficult for Loudoun Unionists and Mosby's supporters.

Mosby realized that the destruction was so great that the area could not support his four hundred men during the coming winter. As soon as the Union cavalry departed, he headed to Petersburg to get Lee's permission to reorganize his command so that half could be sent to the Northern Neck of Virginia, between the Rappahannock and Potomac Rivers. On December 6, his thirty-first birthday, Mosby shared a dinner of leg of lamb with Lee at his headquarters, and he reflected that Grant's headquarters were only about a mile away across the lines. Years later he recalled, "I little dreamed then that I would ever sit down to dinner with Grant: 'What mortal his own doom can guess.'" Lee approved of the transfer to the Northern Neck, and he believed the Rangers could enforce law and order and discourage small enemy raids.

However, Lee could not approve Mosby's proposed reorganization because it was not allowed in army regulations. Mosby wanted to reorganize his seven-company battalion into a regiment of two battalions with himself as colonel and Dolly Richards and William Chapman as battalion commanders, each with a rank of major. Lee recommended he contact Seddon. Mosby presented his plan to Seddon, and he recommended a regiment with Mosby as colonel, with the men divided for the winter under a lieutenant colonel and a major. Mosby agreed and named William Chapman his lieutenant colonel and assigned him to take half of the men to the Northern Neck. All of this became official on January 9, 1865, with Mosby's rank as colonel effective December 7. The command thus officially became the Forty-third Regiment of Virginia Cavalry but never campaigned together as such because Chapman's detachment left on January 3 and remained in the Northern Neck until April 10.

Sheridan never let up in his attempt to capture Mosby or destroy his means of support. A Union cavalry raid under General Alfred Torbert from December 19 to 28 went through Mosby's Confederacy and succeeded in wounding and capturing—momentarily—the Gray Ghost.

A force from Fairfax Court House consisting of a thousand men and horses under Lieutenant Colonel David R. Clendenin, Eighth Illinois Cavalry, rode through Thoroughfare Gap and on December 21 reached the Plains and divided. Clendenin took four hundred men north toward Aldie and sent Major Douglas Frazar, Thirteenth New York Cavalry, west toward Rectortown with six hundred men. He directed Frazar to turn north from Rectortown and ride that evening to Rector's Cross Roads, reuniting with him around midnight in Middleburg. Frazar's column arrived at Rectortown in the early evening and dismounted to make fires and cook supper.

When Mosby received word of Frazar's approach, he was two miles on the other side of Rectortown, at the home of Clotilda Carter, attending the wedding of one of his men, Jacob "Jake" Lavinder, to Judith Edmonds. Without interrupting dinner, Mosby and Thomas R. Love excused themselves and went to reconnoiter. The weather was freezing rain, with the wind making it seem even colder. Mosby and Love saw that Frazar's men had built fires and assumed they were camping for the night. Mosby sent word for his men at the wedding to prepare to harass Frazar's column in the morning, while he and Love rode north toward Rector's Cross Roads to spread news of tomorrow's gathering. Four miles along, they saw a light at Ludwell Lake's house, and Mosby thought of the Lake's home-cooked meals and warm hospitality; he told Love they would stop and eat. Love offered to stand watch outside, but Mosby said there was no danger. He felt so secure that he and Love left their revolvers on their horses, tied at the front gate.

At home were Lud and his two daughters, Sara Lake and Landonia "Donie" Skinner, and Donie's two children asleep upstairs. Donie was married to Ben Skinner, one of the Rangers who had been captured and was being held at the Northern prison camp at Point Lookout in Southern Maryland. She had recently returned from visiting her husband and gave Mosby a report on him.

At about 9:00 p.m., Mosby heard horses, rose from the table, opened the back door and saw the house was surrounded by Union cavalry. Frazar had not camped as expected in Rectortown but had resumed his march, taking the same road Mosby and Love had taken. His advance guard had seen the two horses at the front gate and encircled the house. At that moment, several Union cavalrymen came in the front door. Mosby's new hat, cape and overcoat lay in a corner. The jacket he wore had the two stars of a lieutenant colonel. He raised both hands to cover the insignia and in response to their questions of his name and regiment, responded, "Lieutenant Johnston, Sixth Virginia Cavalry." For the first time since 1862, he was captured. Then a strange thing happened that Pauline believed was a miracle in answer to her prayers, divine intervention invoked by the *Agnus Dei* (Lamb of God) medallion she had hung around his neck when he left for the war.

Suddenly, the horsemen in the backyard began firing their carbines, and a bullet came through a window, striking Mosby in the abdomen. "I am shot!" he shouted, not from pain, for he felt only a stinging sensation, but to create panic. To avoid being shot themselves, the Yankees ran back out the front door, overturning the table and putting out the candle. Mosby's wound was bleeding. He stumbled into the adjoining bedroom, took off his coat with the insignia and stuffed it under a bureau. He then lay down and began to give an imitation of a man about to die. He put his hand to his wound and smeared the blood over his mouth, giving the appearance of a man suffering from a mortal internal wound. He hoped his quick thinking would prevent his capture.

Frazar came in with two other officers and asked who he was. Again he answered, "Lieutenant Johnston, Sixth Virginia Cavalry." Frazar told him he needed to examine the wound, to see whether to take him in, and Mosby had no objection. Frazar found that a bullet had entered the abdomen about two inches below and to the left of the navel, a wound that he felt was mortal. On his way out, he remarked to Ludwell, "He will die in twenty-four hours." One of the other soldiers stripped Mosby of his pants and boots.

It appears that Pauline was sagacious in her later comments. Mosby's deliverance still seems miraculous. The bullet had entered the abdomen but traveled above the fibrous tissue just under the skin and deflected, passing around the abdomen to the right side. Frazar wrongly assumed that the bullet had penetrated the membrane lining the abdominal and pelvic wall, thus entering the viscera, leading to peritonitis, usually resulting in death in twenty-four hours. Surgeons today, familiar with gunshot wounds to the stomach, estimate that only 5 percent of similar gunshot wounds deflect like Mosby's.

As soon as the Yankees left, Lake said, "We have to get Mosby out of here. I don't want my house burned down and that is what they will do if they come back and find him here." Mosby was wrapped in quilts, placed in an ox cart and taken to Aquilla Glascock, about a mile and a half to the southwest. Ranger George Slater was boarding there and helped bring Mosby out of the sleet to lie near the fireplace. Slater had been with Jeb Stuart in May when Stuart had been shot in his abdomen and died twenty-seven hours later. Mosby asked Slater to examine his wound and see if it was similar to Stuart's. Slater did and accurately said that this wound was different, passing around Mosby's body.

The next morning, Mosby's surgeon, William Dunn, administered chloroform and extracted the bullet. Mosby remained in bed, but his men moved him continually. He was still in the area on December 27 when Torbett's cavalry came through on their return march. Sheridan had learned that Mosby had been wounded and told his men to search thoroughly for the downed guerrilla chief. No one in the area would say a word. The next day Frazar came through with three hundred men and checked under every bed and in every chicken coop. Mosby eventually wound up at his mother's home on January 3, 1865.

The wounding of Mosby was one of the most sensational news stories of the war. A rumor in Richmond five days after the event led to a published report in the *Richmond Dispatch*. The *New York Herald* endorsed the story, announcing on December 28 that he was "dead and buried." An editorial in the *Baltimore American* proclaimed, "We hope the report may prove true." On December 29, the *New York Herald* confirmed the death and on the thirtieth published an obituary, "The Fate of Mosby; Death of the Notorious Pirate of the Valley." The writer declared, "Like Morgan, Anderson and other guerrillas of like character, Mosby has met with a dog's death."

For Southerners, the story seemed too exciting to be true. First they heard that Mosby was mortally wounded and dead and then word came that he was alive, having outwitted the Yankee who shot him. Two weeks after the event, when it was reported that he was recovering at his father's farm, Confederate journalists warned that this daring and gallant man would retaliate. "Let the Yankees look out, as he is a military Shylock," declared the *Richmond Whig*, "and will demand of them the debt they owe him, to the last farthing." Ranger Tee Edmonds agreed with Pauline. "Oh! How kind Providence shielded from their demon clutches our Moseby [*sic*]."

The night of the shooting, when Frazar joined Clendenin in Middleburg around a campfire, they examined the wounded officer's hat. "I then immediately knew it must be a field officer," Frazar reported. He showed the hat to Love and seven other prisoners they had captured and asked if it belonged to Mosby. They all stated it was not the colonel's hat. Frazar

Probably the most famous photo of John Singleton Mosby, in his full Confederate colonel's uniform. *Courtesy of the Library of Congress.*

decided that whoever the man was, his wounds were mortal, and when he arrived in Fairfax Court House on December 22, he reported that his men had mortally wounded an unidentified major. Frazar came under intense pressure for allowing Mosby to trick him. Less than two months later, he was court-martialed and found guilty of disobeying orders to correct and return charges against one of his privates. On March 13, 1865, he resigned from the Thirteenth New York Cavalry and accepted an appointment to the U.S. Colored Troops.

CHAPTER 6

No Surrender for Mosby

1865

S heridan hoped that with Mosby away he could prevent raids on the B&O Railroad with a strong infantry picket line on the Winchester and Potomac Railroad and with Colonel Marcus A. Reno's Twelfth Pennsylvania Cavalry posted near Charlestown, West Virginia. Dolly Richards, by now so close a replica of Mosby that Mosby might as well have been present, learned of gaps in the Union line and on the frigid night of January 18 slipped through the lines with more than sixty men and derailed a freight train a mile and a half east of Duffield's in West Virginia. The Rangers acquired canned oysters and other luxuries, including a large shipment of coffee beans, making this the Coffee Raid. Sheridan ordered an investigation and had his troops burn all ferryboats on the Shenandoah River.

By mid-February, Sheridan's cavalry had learned the value of overnight raids and tactics used a year earlier by Meade's men, paralleling those used by Mosby. Guided by a deserter or spy and traveling light with no forage or wheels, going silently with no jangling sabers or other accouterments and refraining from stopping anywhere in Mosby's Confederacy to eat, make coffee or feed their horses, they could surprise Mosby's men and capture them in bed. Merritt was in command of this cavalry corps when two deserters from Mosby's command offered to serve as guides. A squad of one hundred men under Snow went to Upperville to search the houses. Snow took a few men to the home of Richards's father on a nearby farm. Richards and two of his men slept inside. But they had enough warning to hide behind a trap door, while the Yankees searched the house and came up empty. Snow's men in town had "captured" two barrels of liquor, and one-third were drunk. They returned to camp with three prisoners.

As another Union contingent under Gibson arrived in Upperville and headed back into the mountains, Richards had arrived. He had about 43 men against 125 Yankees. But Richards knew the terrain and had his men attack the Union rear guard. In close quarters, the Yankee carbines were no match for the Confederate revolvers. Gibson reported that he was "unable to engage in a melee successfully with an enemy armed with at least two revolvers to the man." When it ended, Richards had freed the prisoners of war, recaptured the horses and killed or wounded 25, captured 64 men and 90 horses. Mosby wrote in a letter after the war, "I have always said it was the most brilliant thing our men ever did."

Two days after the event, Stanton heard the rumor in Washington City that an entire detachment of Sheridan's men had been captured, and then reports came in that night in Sheridan's northern region of responsibility the young Jesse McNeill and a small band of guerrillas had captured Generals Crook and Kelley in Cumberland, Maryland. Stanton telegraphed Grant, "The frequent surprises in Sheridan's command have excited a good deal of observation recently." He asked, "Can you excite more vigilance?" Five days later, Stanton's office sent a message asking for an explanation for recent events. On February 25, two days before Sheridan's troops left the Valley, he reported that his burning raids had been generally successful, but "this party was stampeded, and the whole affair badly managed."

Sheridan stated in his memoirs that when he advanced to Cedar Creek in October 1864, detachments necessary to protect his communications in a "hostile region" depleted his line of battle strength to less than Early's army. This was an exaggeration to justify his retrograde movement, but Mosby declared it "the highest tribute ever paid to the efficiency of my command." In an interview in 1911, he said jokingly that Sheridan had made him "the greatest general in history, not even excepting Caesar, Hannibal or General Grant himself," for Sheridan's statement meant that even though Sheridan "had an army of 94,000 men effective for service, and Early but 15,000, that when these generals met Sheridan's force was no larger than Early's because of the detachments out of action which had to guard attacks and skirmishes from behind." Tongue in cheek, Mosby was laughing that Sheridan had credited him with neutralizing seventy-nine thousand Union soldiers with his three hundred guerrillas.

By the last few months of the war, Union commanders on the Washington City early-warning screen in Northern Virginia had lost so much sleep from

General Winfield Scott Hancock replaced Sheridan as the final Union commander in the Shenandoah Valley and last major antagonist to Mosby. *Courtesy of the Library of Congress.*

Mosby's raids and false alarms that they went on the defensive. Sheridan was succeeded by General Winfield Scott Hancock. In Fairfax County, the Union cavalry appeared to be defending the capital from hostile Indians. They had erected a line of stockades for defense, and when they dared to venture into Mosby's Confederacy, they took strong patrols of six hundred to eight hundred cavalry. Apparently when Sheridan departed the region on February 27, he left no advice to Hancock on how to hunt Mosby's men—or if he did, Hancock ignored it.

Hancock was a friend of Stanton's and did well in protecting the B&O Railroad west of Harpers Ferry, but his counter-guerrilla strategy failed. He decided to send out a force consisting of 1,800 infantry, cavalry and artillery, which crossed the Shenandoah River on March 20 and moved south through Loudoun County. Mosby gathered 128 of his Rangers, who were hovering on the hills in every direction. This would be his last major engagement of the war. He concealed his men in a wooded hollow off the Leesburg Turnpike, near today's Lincoln, and sent out six horsemen as bait. A detachment of the Twelfth Pennsylvania Cavalry under Lieutenant John H. Black came galloping after the decoys. Mosby's men charged, killing nine, wounding twelve and capturing thirteen men and fifteen horses. The Union remnant rode back into town and sought refuge behind the Union infantry, protected by a large hedge. Some of Mosby's men then rode into an infantry volley, losing two killed, six wounded and six captured.

The Union command under Reno traveled for three days through Snickersville, Bloomfield, Upperville and Middleburg, under intense harassment and sniper fire from the Rangers. In Reno's official report, he estimated Mosby's command at five hundred men. A few weeks later, when the war had ended, he asked one of Mosby's officers how many had been in the ambush. "One hundred and twenty eight, all told," the man said. Reno exclaimed, "Twenty eight thousand, you mean!" This was one of the highest compliments Mosby's force-multiplying received—in Reno's memory Mosby's force was expanded over two hundred times! When Hancock received Reno's report, he was mystified that such a strong Union force had accomplished much less than he expected.

On April 5, Mosby organized his eighth and last company under Captain George Baylor. He sent Baylor and his fifty men across the Shenandoah River to attack the Loudoun Rangers near Harpers Ferry. Baylor's company proceeded through the Union pickets, with his lead men in blue overcoats. They found the Loudoun Rangers lounging and fishing. In the ensuing melee, Mosby's men killed two, wounded four and captured sixty-five men and eighty-one horses.

Mosby met with his men on April 10 and divided into two detachments. He took about 100 men and captured a small picket post near Berryville, and he ordered Captain Glascock to take a force of 115 men to capture mules from a wagon train near Burke's Station. Glascock was to be married in a few days and decided that, since Richmond had fallen, the war was over. So he took his force to Salem, dismissed them and went home. Also on April 10, Baylor continued the mission, but when he came to Burke's Station, he found the mules too well guarded. He cancelled the mission and took his men to Arundel's Tavern, which was only about three miles south of the southernmost Union fort at Fairfax Station. While there, the Union commander of the Eighth Illinois Cavalry surprised and routed Baylor's command. A few days later, Baylor apologized for tarnishing the honor of his new command. Baylor had violated the hit-and-run principle when he was within easy striking range of a Union cavalry screen and had gone on the defensive.

During the last year of the war, Mosby hunters had two powerful allies in the Lincoln administration attacking Mosby's command with the weapons of military justice and imprisonment. Stanton and Judge Advocate General Joseph Holt agreed that partisans were felons not entitled to prisoner of war status and regarded it as their duty to bring them to justice since the writ of habeas corpus had been suspended as a wartime emergency. They were already directing the effort to arrest and try Northern civilians accused of disloyalty, and now they worked together to use the system of military commissions to prosecute Mosby's men. These commissions were essentially courts-martial of civilians. In 1866 in *Ex parte Milligan*, the Supreme Court ruled that such military trials of civilians were unconstitutional when civil courts were still functioning.

Some prisoner exchanges continued until the end of the war, but Mosby's Rangers were always discriminated against. On February 6, a group of eighty-seven prisoners from Mosby, White and Kincheloe's commands were transferred from Old Capitol Prison in Washington City to Fort Warren in Boston Harbor. They had to walk through the streets of New York City when changing trains. A large crowd gathered on the sidewalks, and Mosby sergeant Alexander G. Babcock recognized the *New York Tribune* editor Horace Greeley. Babcock raised his manacled arms and shouted, "How are you Horace? What do you think of such treatment of prisoners of war?"

By April 1865, about four hundred of Mosby's men were in various Northern prisons. But the attraction of spoils and adventure still brought in more recruits than he needed. On April 12, William Chapman's force returned from wintering in the Northern Neck. As the war ended, Mosby had between three and four hundred men in a regiment of eight companies. He and his men were winning their guerrilla war and were emotionally unprepared for the end.

Mosby's men had seen him cry only once, standing by the deathbed of Tom Turner at Loudoun Heights. But when he read about Lee's surrender in the *Baltimore American* and realized that the war was over, he broke down and said, "I thought I had sounded the profoundest depth of human feeling, but this is the bitterest hour of my life." He was willing to go to North Carolina to join with Joe Johnston's army, which was still fighting General William T. Sherman.

On April 10, Hancock issued a circular to the public announcing that Confederates should surrender, except "the Guerrilla Chief Mosby is not

Horace Greeley, editor of the *New York Tribune*. Mosby's men taunted him as they marched as prisoners through the streets of New York City. *Author's collection.*

included in the parole." That afternoon, Stanton asked Grant for his opinion: should the same lenient terms given to Lee's army be extended to Mosby's Rangers and others? Stanton was surprised by Grant's answer, that all should be given the same terms, including Mosby. Now backtracking, Hancock had his chief of staff Charles H. Morgan write a letter to Mosby proposing a meeting between Mosby and an officer of equal rank to discuss surrender.

At Winchester, Hancock waited two days. Receiving no reply, on April 13 he issued a second circular, mentioning that Mosby had not replied, and if he did not come in, Hancock's forces were willing to desolate Mosby's supporters. Orders were given, and eight thousand Yankee infantry and cavalry were prepared to devastate Mosby's Confederacy. The raid was called off about 1:00 a.m. on April 15 when Hancock was notified of President Lincoln's assassination.

According to some conspiracy theorists, Mosby was in Washington City at this time, conspiring with John Wilkes Booth to assassinate Lincoln. There is no concrete evidence for this, except for the peripheral fact that Louis Powell (or Payne), who working with Booth, had tried to kill Secretary of State William H. Seward. Powell had once been a Ranger but had deserted.

Mosby was stalling—he was still hoping to join up with Johnston's army. He had sent Channing Smith and four men to Richmond to find out what Lee had to say. Lee had gone to his rented home in Richmond after his surrender at Appomattox. Smith asked the general for advice, and Lee responded, "Give my regards to Colonel Mosby, and tell him that I am under parole, and cannot, for that reason, give him any advice." The Ranger took this in and then asked, "But, General, what must I do?" Now that was a different matter. Lee looked at the youth he had known from before the war and said, "Channing, go home, all you boys who fought with me, and help to build up the shattered fortunes of our old state."

Mosby finally sent a letter to Hancock carried by William Chapman with three other officers. As the four entered Union lines near Winchester, a picket was heard to shout, "Thank God! The war is over. I know the end has come when Mosby's men surrender!" The letter was presented to Hancock, who seemed amazed that the officers did not have the appearance or demeanor of outlaws but were educated and cultured gentlemen. Hancock offered a forty-eight-hour period for Mosby to contact his government and meet him in Millwood, a neutral site.

Hancock had no doubt that Mosby and his whole command would surrender. He then paid Mosby probably the highest compliment by sending not a Union colonel but Brigadier General George H. Chapman to receive the surrender. The meeting went pleasantly, with Confederate and Union officers on opposite sides of a table. Mosby felt honored that Hancock had arranged for a general to accept his surrender. Also, Lincoln's funeral was scheduled for the following day, and Mosby and his men expressed regret over his death. Mosby asked for a forty-eight-hour truce extension to verify that Johnston's army was still in the field. Chapman gave an extension until noon on April 20 and another ten days, if his superiors approved. Hancock was favorably impressed by Mosby's notification that his men were free to surrender individually and several had already done so in Winchester. Hancock was willing to give the additional ten days, but Grant was not. He felt Mosby had been given enough time already. "If Mosby does not avail himself of the present truce, end it and hunt him and his men down." He ordered Hancock, "Guerrillas, after beating the armies of the enemy, will not be entitled to quarter."

Nearly two weeks after General Lee's surrender at Appomattox, Mosby disbanded his Rangers rather than surrender. *Author's collection.*

The second Millwood meeting was quite different from the first. A Union officer of unknown name and rank seated himself at the table, while Mosby and about twenty of his men came in. The officer warned Mosby that if he and his men did not surrender immediately, Hancock's army would destroy Loudoun and Fauquier Counties. Furious, Mosby replied in a loud voice, "Tell General Hancock it is in his power to do it, but I will not accept parole before Joe Johnston has surrendered." With that Mosby and his men rode away.

He called for the last rendezvous of his men at nearby Salem, present-day Marshall, and his Rangers gathered in an open field north of town. It was raining, there was a thick fog and it was cold. Mosby stood on foot beside the road near the field, quietly shaking hands as his men arrived. At about noon, the officers ordered the men to mount and form in line. Mosby rode up and down the line, halted and sat on his horse in front as Chapman and Richards read his farewell address:

Fauquier County, April 21, 1865.
Soldiers—
I have summoned you together for the last time. The vision we cherished of a free and independent country has vanished, and that country is now the spoil of a conqueror.
I disband your organization in preference to surrender to our enemies. I am no longer your commander. After an association of more than two eventful years, I part from you with a just pride in the fame of your achievements and grateful recollections of your generous kindness to myself. And now, at this moment of bidding you a final adieu, accept the assurance of my unchanging confidence and regard. Farewell!

Jno. S. Mosby
Colonel

The men would hold annual reunions in their later years, but Mosby attended only one. It was held almost thirty years later on January 16, 1895, in Alexandria, Virginia, and in his carefully written speech, he compared their suffering at their disbanding to the way the Greek god Prometheus felt when punished by Zeus for attempting to give fire to man. He stated that he would be saying good-bye again to return to San Francisco, and he said, "Life cannot afford a more bitter cup than the one I drained when we parted at Salem, nor any higher reward of ambition that that I received as Commander of the Forty-third Virginia Battalion of Cavalry."

Mosby took six men south with him after the disbandment. When they reached the outskirts of Richmond, they acquired a newspaper telling of Johnston's surrender. Munson reported that several horses were hitched on Franklin Street, ready to be taken. Mosby replied that it was too late: "It would be murder and highway robbery now. We are soldiers, not highwaymen." He disbanded for the second and final time, and they dispersed.

His men surrendered under the terms of Appomattox, but Mosby's protraction had cost him. With Grant's offer withdrawn, Hancock had offered a reward of $2,000 for his capture. For the next several months, Mosby visited his parents and other relatives in and around Central Virginia. "I am an outlaw, and self-preservation is the first law of nature," he told his mother one night as he went out the door. "Mosby Still at Large," reported a *New York Herald* article on May 1, and rumor had him heading for Texas. On May 3, Hancock raised the reward to $5,000, to be paid immediately upon Mosby's apprehension and delivery at any military post.

Pauline Mosby. She stood by her husband, even secretly going to General Ulysses S. Grant to get Mosby an official pardon. *Author's collection.*

By June 13, Mosby and his brother Willie were in the law offices of their relative Charles L. Mosby in Lynchburg. Mosby had been informed that he would receive a pardon. But General John Gregg and a delegation had orders to arrest Mosby and hold him until the War Department decided what to do with him. Mosby had his loaded revolvers at his feet, quietly picked them up and placed them on the table. He declared, "I am the *ultimas Romanorum*. I will not submit to arrest. I will kill the first men who attempt it." He left with his brother and departed Lynchburg.

It was a long and complicated process but had great significance for Mosby's future, for it was the foundation for Mosby's friendship with Grant. Grant learned of Lee's great respect for Mosby, and Mosby knew at the time that Grant had ordered his parole and he was grateful. The parole provided that paroled Confederates would not be disturbed, if they remained at home and obeyed the law. Mosby went to Warrenton in Fauquier County to resume his prewar law practice. He stayed out of trouble until August 10, when he went to Alexandria for business. As he walked along King Street, a crowd formed, arguing whether he was a murderer or a noble cavalier. He and some friends ducked into George Harper's tailor shop at King and

Royal Streets. The crowd pressed from outside, and Mosby was taken into custody and released outside of town after being told not to return. A similar event happened to him in Leesburg on January 8, 1866.

At the beginning of February 1866, Pauline told Mosby she was going to Baltimore with their eldest son, Beverly, to buy furniture. Instead she headed to the White House, hoping that her old family friend from Tennessee, former senator and now President Andrew Johnson, could issue a pardon for her husband. Johnson refused, having a deep hatred for partisan guerrillas, based on his time as wartime governor of Tennessee. Pauline immediately took off to Grant's office. There her reception was completely different. Based on Lee's recommendation, Grant warmly welcomed Mrs. Mosby and her son. He listened sympathetically as she described her husband's problems and said he understood. He took out a blank sheet of paper and in his own hand wrote an order exempting Mosby from military arrest and giving him freedom to travel anywhere in the United States. He handed the note to Pauline and escorted her and her son to the door. That night, in their hotel room, as Bev finished his prayers, he looked up at his mother and said, "Now, momma, may I pray to God to send old Johnson to the devil?" Later, when Grant was president, Mosby told him the story. Grant laughed and said, "A great many would have joined in Beverly's prayer!"

CHAPTER 7

Mosby's Postwar Years

August 1865–May 1916

For Mosby, the years from 1865 to 1872 were the most prosperous of his life. Many people living in Mosby's Confederacy—and even Baltimore merchants—came to him for his legal services. Most of his work was for the railroads that he had until recently been destroying. By August 1865, he had moved his family to Warrenton and opened a law office in the California Building, which had been built with gold-rush money from former Virginia governor and Confederate general "Extra Billy" Smith. People requested his autograph and photo, and they recognized him on the street, in trains and wherever he went. A Mosby look-alike showed up in Philadelphia and Baltimore, and the people gave him a royal welcome—until they found out he was a fake. They laughed that they had been fooled by a counterfeit guerrilla.

By 1867, Mosby made enough money to purchase a house on a four-acre plot on Main Street in Warrenton. In 1871, he made $6,000, when the average worker made only $600. He stayed out of politics until the summer of 1869, when military rule under Reconstruction was about to end in Virginia. The state Conservative Party (later the Democrat Party) that opposed Radical Republican Reconstruction nominated Gilbert C. Walker for governor. When Walker came to speak in Warrenton, Mosby met him at the train station and introduced him at a local rally. In his remarks, Mosby said that Walker stood for civilization while the Republican Party represented "barbarism." Mosby campaigned for Walker and fellow Warrenton attorney James Keith. They both won, and a Conservative

Mosby's home in Warrenton, Virginia, today. His wife, Pauline, passed away here in 1876. *Author's collection.*

state legislature ratified the Fourteenth and Fifteenth Amendments, ending Reconstruction in Virginia.

On March 8, 1870, Mosby was in Richmond lobbying for Keith's nomination for state circuit court judge when he happened upon General Lee and visited him in his hotel room. Lee had been president of Washington College in Lexington, Virginia, since October 1865, and he was embarking on his first and only visit to the South since the end of the war. Lee died seven months later, and it being their last meeting, Mosby described it in his memoirs: "The general was pale and haggard, and did not look like the Apollo I had known in the army." Mosby also met General George Pickett at the hotel, where Pickett asked Mosby to accompany him to Lee's room. Mosby agreed and observed that the meeting was formal, cold and embarrassing. Mosby could not stand it and got to his feet. Pickett and Lee both got to their feet and parted with a brief farewell. Going back down the hall, Pickett burst out bitterly, calling Lee "that old man. He had my division slaughtered at Gettysburg." To which Mosby responded, "Well, it made you immortal."

Due to internal divisions within the Conservative Party, Mosby informed John F. Lewis, a U.S. senator from Virginia, that he wanted to meet President Grant. For several months he had discussed the matter with Keith, who warned that he would pay a severe penalty by separating himself from white Virginians and Southerners. Some in the Conservative Party had joined with the new Liberal Republican Party (national Democrat Party) and were nominating Horace Greeley for president. This pushed Mosby over the edge toward Grant. He wrote to Senator Lewis, who responded that Grant was eager to meet Mosby.

On May 8, 1872, Mosby went to Washington City with the now eleven-year-old Beverly. Later Mosby wrote, "I had never before been in the White House. When I walked in with my son into the room where Grant was sitting, his presence inspired something of the awe that a Roman provincial must have felt when first entering the palace of the Caesars. His manner soon relieved me of embarrassment and restored my self-confidence."

Afterward he took the Aquia Creek steamboat back to Alexandria. While on board, he met former Confederate cavalry general Wade Hampton and became so engrossed in describing his visit that he missed Alexandria and only noticed the bell as they passed Mount Vernon.

The visit was a sensation that returned the former Confederate Partisan colonel back to the spotlight. Southerners were shocked. They saw Grant as the head of the pro–African American, anti–Southern Republican Party. By endorsing him, it was felt that Mosby was betraying the legitimacy of the recent Rebellion. Mosby himself said that the South would not have been more shocked if during the war he had deserted to the Union side. Grant considered Mosby to be someone who could sway the votes of Virginia conservatives and moderates and an emotional link to the glory days of the recent war.

In his memoirs, Grant wrote:

> *Since the close of the war I have come to know Colonel Mosby personally, and somewhat intimately. He is different entirely from what I had supposed. He is slender, not tall, wiry, and looks as if he could endure any amount of physical exercise. He is able, thoroughly honest and truthful. There were probably but few men in the South who could have commanded successfully a separate detachment in the rear of an opposing army, and so near the border of hostilities, as long as he did without losing his entire command.*

In a speech in Boston on April 27, 1906, Mosby said of Grant, "No man ever had a better friend than he was to me."

Political poster for the 1872 presidential campaign. Mosby's support of Ulysses S. Grant made him *persona non grata* in his native Virginia. *Author's collection.*

Mosby had promised to support Grant in Virginia and predicted that Grant would carry the state if he successfully persuaded Congress to enact the Amnesty Bill then under consideration. Congress had already removed the political disabilities of many former Confederates, and soon the bill was passed and most of the remaining Rebels were pardoned. Mosby went home and began enlisting politicians in Virginia as "Grant's Conservatives." It was a crusade that put him in the role of Grant's guerrilla warrior in Virginia. His main disciple was John S. Wise, former Confederate captain and son of former Virginia governor Henry S. Wise. With John Wise and a few others, Mosby attended the Democratic Convention in Baltimore in July.

He supported a "straight Democrat," meaning anyone other than Greeley. When the convention voted for Greeley as expected, Mosby was there to shepherd the disgruntled Virginians into the Grant camp.

He invited voters in Fauquier County to a debate between himself and his friend Eppa Hunton for Grant and Greeley, respectively. He arranged the meeting not in Warrenton but in Salem, where he had disbanded his men. It was symbolic of his return to battle, and no one who saw or heard him that day could argue that he was not again on the attack, now as a stump speaker. "Mosby Makes a Raid on Greeley," blared one headline. Hunton had been wounded as a colonel leading his men at Pickett's Charge and was later promoted to general. He had a law office in Warrenton in the same building as Mosby and was himself running as a Conservative for the House of Representatives. He would win and go on to a career in the House and U.S. Senate and continue as Mosby's friend.

News of the debate spread quickly, and that evening, Mosby heard what had been said at a Greeley rally in Warrenton. It was there that John B. Withers, former Confederate army private and now mayor, had said, "Colonel Mosby might drive Confederate generals, but he couldn't drive a Confederate private into supporting Grant!" Mosby confronted Withers, and their argument became so heated that Judge Keith had them arrested and set their bail at $4,000 each. When it was announced that Grant had carried Virginia in November, Mosby wired the White House: "Virginia casts its vote for Grant, peace and reconciliation." Grant had carried the state by two thousand votes, mainly because many white voters stayed home and left the vote to a minority of Republicans and Grant's Conservatives. There are divided opinions on how much Mosby's support actually helped Grant in Virginia.

Mosby admitted that Grant gave him more credit than he deserved. A few days after the election, he was in Washington City on business, waiting in the outer office of the treasury secretary, when in walked Grant. He shook Mosby's hand and said, "I heard you were here and came to thank you for getting the vote of Virginia." He offered to appoint Mosby to a federal job, but Mosby refused. He realized that accepting a position would make him a scalawag, a Southerner who cooperated with the Radical Republicans for private gain, and weaken his position as Grant's ambassador to Conservatives in Virginia, just as accepting spoils in the war would have weakened him as a guerrilla chief.

By 1874, the Conservative Party was in control in Virginia and wanted to have nothing to do with Mosby's attempts to unite with the Grant administration. Hunton was running for reelection to the House, and Mosby wanted to oppose him. In June, Mosby was in Salem and met up with B.F. Rixey, a former state senator. Their verbal argument turned to blows, hitting each other with canes and carriage whips. Friends separated them, and Mosby realized that his candidacy would be a losing cause. He threw his support behind to his friend James Barbour, a Culpeper attorney.

Mosby's "raid" against Hunton incurred the wrath of Alexander D.F. Payne, another Warrenton attorney. Payne began exhibiting a document that accused Mosby of duplicity and deceit in attempting to subvert the Conservative Convention. On August 20, a week before the convention, Mosby challenged Payne to a duel; Payne accepted, selecting squirrel rifles at forty paces and a spot in Fauquier County. What followed was a fiasco and sensation for the newspapers. Mosby wanted the place to be in Prince Georges County, Maryland, opposite Alexandria, but Payne wanted to duel at Buckland Tavern in Prince William County. When Judge Keith heard of this, he had Payne arrested and sent detectives to Washington City, where they surrounded and captured Mosby in the lobby of the Congressional Hotel. Mosby returned home, where he and Payne apologized.

Mosby was now a man without a party. "I lost the confidence of both but preserved my integrity and self-respect," he later wrote. He still got what he wanted most: a relationship with Grant that gave him informal personal power. But he paid a high price. Southern political leaders asked him for secret political favors from Grant, but if it became public knowledge, they would withdraw and apologize for contacting that "odious man from Virginia." On May 2, 1875, he wrote Grant that he had become so loathsome in the public eye that he could no longer visit the White House. Most of his law business dried up, and he had to borrow money.

Mosby's main support was his loving and understanding wife, Pauline. Writing to a friend during the 1872 campaign, she enclosed one of Grant's speeches and a clipping of a favorable newspaper editorial, "which Mr. Mosby says more than compensates him for all the abuse he has heaped on him by the Greeleyites." The couple remained close, and he cooperated in educating their children in Roman Catholic schools, sending May and Beverly to boarding school in Montreal. Immediately after the war, they welcomed Mosby's sisters Blakely and Lucy to live in their home, and Pauline continued having children, giving birth eight times in eighteen years. Their last child, Alfred M., was born March 9 and died June 30, 1876. Pauline never recovered from Alfred's birth, and she died of complications from childbirth on May 10, 1876, at the age of thirty-nine. A large crowd gathered for her funeral, and Mosby had carved on

Pauline Mosby's gravestone in Warrenton, Virginia. The graves of some of her eight children are behind her. *Author's collection.*

her tombstone a quotation from the eulogy of the priest at her funeral mass: "She died as she lived, a faithful Catholic."

Mosby grieved, and he would never remarry. On the political front, he was losing his mentor Grant, who was soon ending his second term. After the Republican convention, he met with Grant and announced he was supporting the party nominee, Rutherford B. Hayes, another former Union general. On July 24, he sent a letter to Hayes, carefully written, in which he claimed to be one of the Conservative class in Virginia who would vote for Hayes if he made a friendly overture to the South. The letter was completely in line with the goal of Hayes's Southern policy, which was to win the votes of Southern white Democratic/Conservatives who had been Whigs and Douglas Democrats before the Rebellion. Mosby had avoided becoming a member of the Republican Party, but he announced that he was going to do what he had said would ruin him: he was joining the Republicans. He even endorsed the political equality of the races. The Democratic Party, still called the Conservative Party in Virginia, believed in white supremacy and condemned the Republicans as the party of black people; in its eyes, Mosby was a traitor. He knew it and wrote, "I know very well the measure of denunciation which the expression of these sentiments will receive from the people in whose cause I shed my blood and sacrificed the prime of my life. Be it so. I wait on time for my vindication."

Some Southern Conservatives responded to Hayes's appeal, but Democratic candidate Samuel J. Tilden carried Virginia easily and won the national popular vote by 250,000. But there were disputed returns from several states, and an electoral commission named Hayes the winner. The people of Warrenton avoided Mosby and his family as if they were stricken with an infectious disease. No one dared insult Mosby, but his children were greeted with heckling and catcalls whenever they left their home. Someone did take a potshot at him at the Warrenton train station. His income decreased by 80 percent, and by November 21, 1876, he had moved his law office to Washington City and had shut up his house, taking his children to live with his mother. When he returned to Warrenton for court days, he carried a loaded revolver on his hip. In 1878, he sold the house to Eppa Hunton.

Mosby did accept an appointment from President Hayes, and on February 2, 1879, he arrived in Hong Kong harbor as American consul. As a British colony, Hong Kong had the protection of the British flag and was expanding as the commercial center of China. As consul, Mosby was to perform legal functions for U.S. citizens and businesses, but his main duty was to supervise and facilitate American commerce. The consul served as special counsel for U.S. sailors and shipmasters. He signed seamen onto American flagships and approved their discharge from the crews of ships. If a shipmaster had been cruel to a seaman, the consul could discharge the seaman from the ship; if a seaman had misbehaved or fallen ill, the captain could have the consul remove him. For U.S. seamen stranded in port, the consul was to provide lodging, clothing and passage home.

For years, many American consuls were not paid a salary but were expected to live from "unofficial fees." Eventually, they were robbing the U.S. treasury of official revenues. Almost everywhere, American merchants went to the British consul for help, knowing that the U.S. consul was either absent, worthless or a thief. Mosby reported that ship captains in the Far East had the impression that each U.S. consul made his own law and noted that in Hong Kong the stealing of fees was worth more than a bonanza in Nevada. One of the greatest abuses involved the care of discharged seamen. Regulations required the consul to collect three months' extra wages for a discharged crewman and, if a U.S. citizen, give him two-thirds and deposit one-third in an account for the aid of destitute seamen. From this account, the consul was to provide for the man's living expenses and his passage home. The previous consul, David H. Bailey, friend of Treasury Secretary John Sherman, had deposited these funds in his own account and had not only stolen the extra wages of U.S. seamen but had also collected and kept the three months' extra wages due sailors of other nationalities discharged from U.S. ships. Before three weeks had passed, Mosby reported to the State Department that, based on two court cases, he had excluded foreign nationals from contributing to the destitute fund and was giving them all their extra wages. He gave each U.S. sailor his two-thirds and placed one-third in the consular account designated for destitute seamen. Word spread that an honest man had taken over in Hong Kong.

As he implemented his reform programs in Hong Kong, the *China Mail* praised him for cleaning out the utter rottenness in the system. "The gallant Colonel has apparently adopted as his motto the well-worn words, *Fiat justitia, ruat coelum*, Latin for 'let justice be done though the heavens should fall.'" His best time was in 1879, when Grant, now retired and on a world tour, visited Hong Kong with his wife, Julia, and eldest son, Fred. At breakfast one morning, the ex-president told of a trip by donkey from Jaffa to Jerusalem.

"That was the roughest road I ever traveled," he said.

"General, you traveled one rougher road than that," reminded Mosby.

"Where?" asked Grant.

"From the Rapidan to Richmond."

Grant chuckled. "I guess there were more obstructions in the road," he agreed.

Mosby's consulship ended in March 1885 with the inauguration of Democrat president Grover Cleveland. Supposing he would not be reappointed, he sent a letter to Grant, asking that he help him locate employment. July came, and Mosby prepared to return to the United States. The day before leaving, he received word that his presidential friend had died. But even in the last days, as cancer ate away at him, Grant had not forgotten his Rebel friend who had gone against Southern popular thought to bring Grant political support in Virginia. When he was once asked about whether he believed that war is hell, Mosby had responded, "Hell is being a Republican in Virginia!"

One of Grant's last pieces of correspondence was a letter to the railway builder and executive Leland Stanford, who had been governor of California in 1861 and helped keep the state in the Union. When Mosby stepped ashore in San Francisco, carrying with him a silver loving cup given to him in appreciation by Chinese merchants, he was notified

John Mosby as American consul in Hong Kong. President Rutherford B. Hayes sent him as far from Virginia as possible. *Courtesy of the Library of Congress.*

by Stanford that an attorneyship with the Southern Pacific railroad awaited him. He was also offered a contract from a lecture bureau in Massachusetts to speak in New England on the inside story of his amazing military activities. He accepted and began the strenuous schedule of a speaking tour. This led to another offer, and his talks were soon being published in the *Boston Herald*. By 1887, the newspaper series had been compiled in a book titled *Mosby's Reminiscences*.

During this time, former Confederate general Marcus Wright, who assisted in editing *The War of the Rebellion: A Compilation of the Official Records of the Union and Confederate Armies*, wrote to Mosby, "It may and I know will be interesting to you that I have carefully read all of General R.E. Lee's dispatches, correspondence, etc., during the war of 1861–1865; and while he was not in the habit of paying compliments, yet these papers of his will show that you received from him more compliments and commendations than any other officer in the Confederate army."

Other volumes came from Mosby's pen. Since the end of the war, many former Confederates had laid the defeat at Gettysburg at the feet of his former commander, J.E.B. Stuart. Mosby wrote two volumes in Stuart's defense: *Stuart's Cavalry Campaigns* and *Stuart's Cavalry in the Gettysburg Campaign*. The latter book was based on the *Official Records* and caused other former Rebel leaders, especially Jubal A. Early, to answer him sharply. Shortly after Mosby's death, *The Memoirs of Col. John S. Mosby* was published.

While working as a lawyer for the railroad, Mosby visited a Virginia family that had moved to Southern California. He got to mentor their young son, Georgie, whose grandfather and great-uncles had been Confederate officers in the war. As a young boy, Georgie would kneel beside his mother's chair to recite his bedtime prayers. On the wall behind her hung two small portraits he thought were of God the Father and Jesus Christ, the former a somber man with white hair and beard, the latter portrait a younger man with dark hair and beard. He looked upon these faces as he prayed. Only later did he realize that these men were not the Father and the Son. They were Generals Robert E. Lee and Stonewall Jackson.

Georgie grew up hearing tales of daring raids and stunning cavalry attacks from the Gray Ghost himself. During visits, Mosby would reenact the Civil War with Georgie; playing himself, he let Georgie play the part of General Lee as they would recount the battles of the war astride their horses. That Virginia family was the Patton family, and the young man eventually went on to attend Virginia Military Institute and West Point, becoming the acclaimed general of the Third Army in Europe, George S. Patton Jr. George Smith Patton, Patton's grandfather, was a Confederate colonel. He was killed at the Third Battle of Winchester during the Valley Campaign of 1864. A younger brother, Colonel Waller Tazewell Patton, died of mortal wounds suffered during Pickett's Charge in the Battle of Gettysburg. Four other brothers were also officers in the Confederate States Army: Colonel John Mercer Patton, Colonel Isaac Patton, Lieutenant James F. Patton and Lieutenant Hugh Mercer Patton.

General Patton was one of the pivotal figures of World War II. His bold, aggressive, no-holds-barred combat style reflected his unique understanding that tanks were the cavalry of modern warfare. His successful command proved to be a differentiating element in the Allies' victory in Europe. In a study of General Patton, one must wonder where he got his understanding of mobile warfare and how he was able to go toe-to-toe with German field marshal Erin Rommel and come out on top. Could it be that what gave him an edge and the advantage was some of the lessons he learned riding with

General George S. Patton, commander of the Third Army in World War II. His use of tanks as armored cavalry was possibly influenced by the time he spent during his youth in California, riding with Mosby. *Courtesy of the Library of Congress.*

the Gray Ghost? Through Patton, Mosby's innovative style in using guerrilla warfare probably had a profound impact on the outcome of World War II.

In the early 1890s, on one of his well-spaced visits to his family back in Virginia, Mosby received an unexpected and conspicuous honor. Virginia's famous sculptor Edward V. Valentine, who had prepared the recumbent statue of Robert E. Lee in Lee Chapel in Lexington, Virginia, made a bust of the raider. In appreciation, Mosby presented him with his plumed campaign hat. This hat, the one he had worn when he was wounded at the Lake house, had been returned to him by the niece of the Federal officer in charge of the raid.

When the equestrian statue of General Lee was unveiled on Monument Avenue in Richmond on May 29, 1890, Mosby was among the honored guests invited. He refused the invitation, although his Rangers were there in a body and created considerable attention. One cause of his reluctance to attend was the presence of former General Early, to whom he had taken a considerable dislike since the end of the war.

In January 1895, Mosby did attend the first reunion of the Forty-third Battalion, held in Alexandria, Virginia. More than 150 Rangers attended,

Unveiling of the Lee statue on Monument Avenue in Richmond in 1890. Mosby was invited but refused to come from California to attend. *Author's collection.*

many shaking the hand of their former commander—who was now sixty-two, graying and fuller in body—for the first time since their final meeting in Salem. Several who came, like Sam Chapman, had temporarily exchanged their pulpit broadcloth for their Confederate gray. This led Mosby to comment, "Well boys, if you fight the devil like you fought the Yankees, there will be something to record Judgment Day."

The reunion reached its climax at a banquet, an affair that developed into an all-out crying fest. An address by Mosby started the tears. In his talk, the lawyer went back to Salem for a theme and was himself so overcome with emotion he never again attended an assembly of his men. The greatest pang was elicited by these words:

> *Your presence here this evening recalls our last parting. I see the line drawn up to hear the last order I ever gave you. I see the moistened eyes and quivering lips. I hear the command to break ranks. I feel the grasp of the hands and see the tears on the cheeks of men who had dared death so long it had lost its terror. And I know now, as I knew then, that each heart suffered with mine the agony of the Titan in his resignation to fate.*

Modern skepticism has destroyed one of the most beautiful creations of Epic ages, the belief that the spirits of dead warriors meet daily in the halls of Valhalla, and there around the festive board recount the deeds they did in the other world. For this evening, at least, let us adopt the ancient superstition, if superstition it be. It may seem presumptuous to me, but a man who belonged to my command may be forgiven for thinking that, in that assembly of heroes, when the feast of the wild boar is spread, Smith and Turner, Montjoy and Glasscock, Fox and Whitescarver, and all their comrades, will not be unnoticed in the mighty throng.

One more narrow escape from death faced Mosby. While visiting a friend in Charlottesville in April 1897, he leaned over the dashboard of the buggy he was riding in to lift the horse's tail from the reins. The animal became frightened and kicked out with its nailed hoof, striking the lawyer in the head. Passersby lifted him from the dusty street, bleeding profusely from his forehead. They took him to the University of Virginia hospital, where he lay unconscious for days. It was revealed that his skull was fractured, and he could no longer use his left eye.

Coming up from Richmond was one of the best-known surgeons of the South, Dr. Hunter McGuire, who had recently founded the College of Physicians and Surgeons, now part of the Medical College of Virginia (MCV), Virginia Commonwealth University. (During the war, the medical college had remained open and graduated a class every year throughout the conflict. MCV is the only Southern medical school still in existence to have done so.) McGuire had also been Stonewall Jackson's physician. He entered the sick room and found an intern beside the bed.

"Is he conscious?" asked the surgeon.

"I'll see," replied the intern. He leaned over the prostrate form, putting his mouth close to the bandaged face.

"What's your name?"

Quickly, the victim's lips moved. "None of your damned business."

"He's conscious all right," said McGuire, taking off his coat and rolling up his sleeves.

With careful treatment, the danger passed and his body began to heal. But Mosby could never again depend on his keen eyesight. He was forced to wear glasses and take afternoon naps. In April 1898, at sixty-four, Mosby offered to raise a battalion or regiment for the war in Cuba but was turned down.

In 1899, Winston Churchill wrote *The River War* about his experiences as a young officer in the Sudan. Churchill had survived the Battle of Omdurman in 1898 by following Mosby's advice to fight with a revolver rather than a

Dr. Hunter McGuire, Stonewall Jackson's physician during the war. He came from Richmond to Charlottesville in 1896 to attend Mosby after his serious accident. *Author's collection.*

sword, and he testified in his book to the efficacy of Mosby's cavalry tactics. Churchill advocated arming all British troops with revolvers and doing away with outmoded lances and sabers. Mosby, according to Churchill, was a soldier ahead of his time. Taking note of the then little-known Churchill's support for Mosby's practices in his book, the *Baltimore News* and the *Richmond Dispatch* commented in 1902 that Mosby's "career is full of much that is valuable to the military historian." Might the history of the twentieth century have been very different if Churchill had ridden into the fray with a sword and not with a Mauser pistol?

In 1901, the Southern Pacific railway underwent a sudden reorganization. Left in its wake was the old Ranger. Once again, his political connections came to his rescue. In July, President William McKinley appointed him as a special agent of the General Land Office. For three years, he worked at his new assignment with headquarters in Sterling, Colorado, spending much of his time on the trail of cattle barons who were fencing land illegally in Nebraska, Colorado and Alabama. Then in 1904, President Theodore Roosevelt, listening to the pleas of some of Mosby's friends, named him assistant attorney to the Department of Justice.

The years following 1904 were not kind to Mosby. A characteristic at this time was a bad disposition, perhaps the aftermath of his days as a military leader. He talked fast and expected his orders to be obeyed just as promptly as he had in the war. At times he was an intolerant, irascible old man, rude to those who bothered him. One of his sons said, "The war ruined a good father." During and after the war, his life had been above average, first as a partisan leader and then as a lawyer, American Consul and railroad attorney. Now he was bound to a swivel chair, surrounded by young men and women who only knew of his war record as hearsay.

But behind all his peculiarities and social violations, Mosby had one trait that he kept from his years as a leader: until his dying day, he kept a personal and paternal interest in his men. Hearing that one of them was in financial difficulty, he took it upon himself to make sure the fellow's son got a responsible job, reminding the young man as he prepared for work that he must send part of his salary to his father. He frequently shared with others money he himself needed more. And he kept spending long hours in study to be better able to defend the campaigns of his long-dead friend and hero, Jeb Stuart.

New inventions, like the automobile and football, left him resentful toward them in that they disturbed or made more out-of-date the historical setting of the war. His thinking advanced with his years, but his habits and way of life remained in the 1860s. The war period was the hub around which revolved the half-century span of his later life. As the years passed and the ranks of his veterans thinned, he felt the separation from his old battalion. "I am beginning to feel very lonely in this world now," he once remarked. "Nearly all of my friends are gone, and I have made no new ones."

Deaths of students resulting from football injuries at the University of Virginia prompted him in 1909 to write authorities at his old school, protesting that football was "murder." In 1910, Mosby made a peaceful raid into New England, back on the lecture trail. His purpose was to help a boys' charitable cause and to augment his own dwindling finances. The Associated Press had announced his ouster from the Justice Department without cause and stated that Mosby was in poverty. "I was up against it during the war and did not take it seriously to heart," the press service quoted him. "I shall endeavor not to do so now." His discharge from the government had followed a change of administration, though it may have been predicated on his age. He was nearly seventy-seven, and his hair was now white. But his cheeks were still rosy, his appetite good and his step quick. He showed his age only in attenuation and general frailty.

His next four years were spent in quiet and periodical work on his memoirs. At this time he remarked, "I pitched my politics in too high a key when I voted for Grant. I ought to have accepted office under him. My family would now be comfortably supplied with money."

But those who remembered his staunch political sentiments knew these words did not come from the heart. He offered his services to King George V of Great Britain as the Great War began in 1914 and took a dim view of President Woodrow Wilson.

As Mosby's work on his memoirs neared an end, a delegation one day brought a token of appreciation from the university that had expelled him

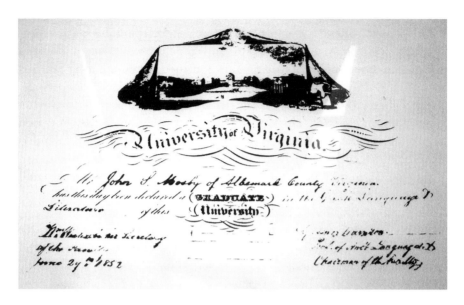

This recently discovered diploma was given to Mosby after two years at the University of Virginia. Since he did not complete the full four-year course, many believe he never graduated from the university. *Courtesy of the Stuart-Mosby Cavalry Museum.*

in 1853. It consisted of a bronze medal and an embossed address of the affection and esteem of his friends and admirers at the University of Virginia:

> *Your friends and admirers in the University of Virginia welcome this opportunity of expressing for you their affection and esteem, and congratulating you upon the vigor and alertness both of body and mind with which you have rounded out your four-score years.*
>
> *Your Alma Mater has pride in your scholarly application in the days of your youth, in your martial genius manifested in a career singularly original and romantic, in the forceful fluency of the history made by yourself and your comrades in the Army of Northern Virginia and in the dignity, diligence, and sagacity with which you have served your reunited country at home and abroad.*
>
> *Endowed with the gift of friendship, which won for you the confidence of both Lee and Grant, you have proven yourself a man of war, a man of letters, and a man of affairs worthy of the best traditions of your University and your State, to both of which you have been a loyal son.*
>
> *University of Virginia*
> *January 28, 1915*

He refused to attend the actual award ceremony, responding to University President Edwin A. Alderman, "The reason I didn't go was that they intended to give me a testimonial that would be an atonement for their having expelled me from the University for shooting a bully. That determined me not to go. It is crucifixion to me to undergo any kind of a ceremonial."

He considered it a "pardon" for a guilty offender, reminding him of his jail sentence and expulsion. After the event, which had included former president William Howard Taft, Alderman sent the medal and testimonial signed by the faculty, and Mosby saw that he had responded correctly—these were atonements for the expulsion.

Then the University Colonnade Club invited him to speak on campus about his war remembrances for an honorarium of $150, and he felt this struck the right tone—this was a true honor for a worthy alumnus who did not need to be pardoned—he accepted immediately. He wrote to his grandson, Mosby Campbell, "I didn't mind going to Canada and New York—but I shed my blood for her people [Virginia] and you know what I got in return. It is too late for them to atone for it now. It is, however, very gratifying for my old men to go there and greet me."

His talk was on May 1, 1915, and Cabell Hall was packed. On stage he was joined by nine of his Rangers, including William Chapman, Dolly Richards and surgeon William Dunn, who had in his pocket the lancet he had used to cut the bullet from Mosby over fifty years before at Glascock's. Alderman introduced him, and his talk was well received. He knew the invitation to speak about himself was a request not to criticize Lee, like he usually did in his talks in the North when he defended Stuart. He complied, and nothing spoiled the harmonious spirit of the occasion.

For his University of Virginia talk, he excluded the press. He was finished with controversy and wanted to view himself as a symbol of reconciliation between the North and South. Back home in Washington City after his talk, he wrote, "One of the first things I said to [my grandson] Stuart was that for the first time in my life I felt like a rich man—that the kindness and consideration shown me where I was raised and educated convinced me that I possessed something that gold could not buy and that I have not lived in vain."

To another grandson—Spotswood—he wrote, "The reception I got at the University is the proudest recollection of my life." He sealed the reconciliation nearly six months later by donating to the university fifty copies of Jeb Stuart's congratulatory order on the Stoughton Raid.

By the end of 1915, Mosby was confined to his home by general debility. In three months he was at Garfield Hospital in Washington City. The end came at

This medal was given to Mosby from the University of Virginia in 1915. *Courtesy of the Stuart-Mosby Cavalry Museum.*

9:00 a.m. on May 30, 1916. He was conscious almost to the last. As he uttered his last breath, one of his daughters said the baptismal words of the Roman Catholic Church—the church of his wife, the church he admired but never fully embraced—and sprinkled the holy water on him. Hopefully his beloved wife, Pauline, was waiting for him, ready to plead his case to the Almighty.

Mosby's grave in Warrenton, Virginia, is next to his wife's grave and close to the graves of many of his men. *Author's collection.*

His body was moved to Warrenton by train on the morning of June 1. On board as pallbearers and bodyguards were Fount Beattie and other Rangers. Along, too, were the Alexandria, Culpeper and Charlottesville units of the National Guard. At the station, joined by the Warrenton Rifles, the uniformed troops formed line beside the station and trod behind a black hearse to the town hall, where the body lay in state for several hours. Then the coffin was carried to the cemetery, a few blocks away.

An open grave waited near an obelisk marking the mound under which lay bodies of five hundred Confederate comrades. Close by were the graves of Pauline, their two sons who had died in infancy and the fairly fresh grave where rested John Junior, his war baby, buried the preceding August. So John Singleton Mosby—lawyer, soldier, patriot and author—was buried in appropriate company, on the brow of a hill, overlooking a town and countryside he had ridden through during the war and where he had lived several years afterward.

The editorial response to Mosby's death from the *Richmond Virginian* proclaimed, "With the bitterness of war all gone, there remains to Americans,

North and South, a precious heritage of valor, of self-sacrifice, of sturdy, unflagging never-give-up spirit, a heritage which, in future days of possible stress, will prove inspiration unto us." University of Virginia president Alderman issued a statement, saying, "The University of Virginia lost one of her bravest and noblest sons. The president and the faculty send expression of most profound sympathy and affection." Eulogies published across the nation outlined his war career, praised his fighting spirit and mentioned the coincidence of his death on Memorial Day.

Less than three years after Mosby's death, the people of Warrenton organized a campaign to erect a monument. In March 1919, the *Confederate Veteran* published an appeal for donations to honor "one of Virginia's bravest, most gallant heroes," who "must not be forgotten—no, not by our children's children." The fund drive succeeded, and a twenty-five-foot granite monument was erected on the lawn next to the Fauquier County courthouse. For the dedication on June 19, 1920, people filled the sidewalks and stood in the windows of nearby buildings. A few of his Rangers attended, and the poem "Mosby," by Beverly R. Tucker, was read, which closed:

> *And when the children gather round*
> *Your knee at twilight hour,*
> *Tell them of Mosby and his men—*
> *Of Southern knighthood's flower.*

His granddaughter Pauline pulled the cord, and the monument was unveiled.

The Gray Ghost was famous beginning with the capture of General Stoughton and, by the end of the war, was among the most popular Confederate heroes. He continued to attract attention and hero worship wherever he went, but his popularity did slump after he campaigned for Grant in 1872 and did not recover until 1900. Then Southerners began speaking positively of him again, and he became the subject of three silent films, one featuring Mosby playing himself. At the time of his death, eulogies exalted him as the most famous Confederate raider, a guerrilla who defied death innumerable times, skillfully bedeviling his Northern foes, and made his name a terror to children. Southerners eventually overlooked his Republicanism, and he reappeared among the South's most popular military personalities and the most famous non-general officer. His tactics influenced future military and political leaders, such as General George S. Patton and Winston Churchill, and are still relevant today.

This monument to Mosby is near the Old Courthouse in Warrenton, Virginia. It was raised by donations just a few years after his death. *Author's collection.*

In 1971, the Fauquier National Bank in Warrenton dedicated its area for public concerts Mosby Plaza. The Little River Turnpike that straddles Loudoun and Fauquier Counties in Northern Virginia was redesignated John S. Mosby Highway in 1980. Today, Mosby is a popular subject for Civil War paintings and collectibles. He is held in such high regard that noted historians believe Mosby was a general, even though his highest rank was colonel. In 1990, it was written in Ken Burns' book *The Civil War: An Illustrated History*, "On March 9, 1863, General John Singleton Mosby's Confederate Rangers raided Fairfax Court House, Virginia." In 1995, Historical Sculptures of Cairo, New York, advertised miniature busts of eight Civil War heroes by sculptor Ron Tunison. They were Lincoln, Custer and Chamberlain for the Union and Lee, Jackson, Stuart, Forrest and Mosby for the Confederacy. The Bradford Exchange sells a "Porcelain Civil War Art Knife Collection," which includes one blade devoted to General Mosby. James L. Swanson, in his best-selling book, *Manhunt* says, "On the morning of [Lincoln's] funeral, [Stanton] sent a message to General Hancock at Winchester retracting his flirtation about enlisting Confederate General Mosby in the manhunt." If there could be an entity that bestowed honorary generalships like universities give honorary doctorates, Mosby would be number one on the list. In the public mind, Mosby's support of President Grant only makes him a more interesting and controversial figure. In the mind of Civil War enthusiasts, Mosby is near the top of the Confederate pantheon.

The Scout Toward Aldie

By Herman Melville, author of *Moby Dick*

The following are the first and last three verses of a 114-verse poem based on the three days Melville spent chasing Mosby with Union cavalry in Northern Virginia in April 1864.

The cavalry-camp lies on the slope
Of what was late a vernal hill,
But now like a pavement bare—
An outpost in the perilous wilds
Which ever are lone and still;
But Mosby's men are there—
Of Mosby best beware.

Great trees the troopers felled, and leaned
In antlered walls about their tents;
Strict watch they kept; 'twas Hark! and Mark!
Unarmed none cared to stir abroad
For berries beyond their forest-fence:
As glides in seas the shark,
Rides Mosby through green dark.

All spake of him, but few had seen
Except the maimed ones or the low;
Yet rumor made him every thing—
A farmer—woodman—refugee—
The man who crossed the field but now;
A spell about his life did cling—
Who to the ground shall Mosby bring?

———◆••◆◆•◆———

The amber sunset flushed the camp
As on the hill their eyes they fed;
The picket dumb looks at the wagon dart;
A handkerchief waves from the bannered tent—
As white, alas! The face of the dead:
Who shall the withering news impart?
The bullet of Mosby goes through heart to heart!

They buried him where the lone ones lie
(Lone sentries shot on midnight post)—
A green-wood grave-yard hid from ken,
Where sweet-fern flings an odor nigh—
Yet held in fear for the gleaming ghost!
Though the bride should see threescore and ten,
She will dream of Mosby and his men.

Now halt the verse, and turn aside—
The cypress falls athwart the way;
No joy remains for bard to sing;
And heaviest dole of all is this,
That other hearts shall be as gay
As hers that now no more shall spring:
To Mosby-land the dirges cling.

Mosby's Recommendation from Jeb Stuart

Hd.Qtrs. Cav. Div. Army of N. Va.
Mar. 25, 1863

Dear Captain [Mosby],
I enclose your evidence of appointment by the President in the Provisional Army of the Confederate States—You will perceive by Gen. Lee's accompanying instructions that you will be continued in your present sphere of conduct and enterprise, and already a Captain, you will proceed to organize a band of permanent followers for the war—but by all means ignore the term "Partizan Ranger." It is in bad repute. Call your command "Mosby's Regulars," and it will give it a tone of meaning and solid worth which all the world will soon recognize, and you will inscribe that name of a fearless band of heroes on the pages of our country's history and enshrine it in the hearts of a grateful people. Let "Mosby's Regulars" be a name of pride with friends and respectful trepidation with enemies. You will have to be very much on your guard against incorporating in your command deserters from other branches of the service. Insist upon the most unequivocal evidence of honorable discharge in all cases. Non-conscripts under and over age will be very advantageous. Their entry into service must be unconditional, except that you are their Captain and their Lieutenants are to be chosen by the men provided no unworthy man be so chosen. As there is no time within which you are required to raise this command, you ought to be very fastidious in choosing your men and make them always stand the test of battle, and temptation to neglect duty before acceptance. I was greatly obliged to you for the saddle of Stoughton…

We must have that unprincipled scoundrel Wyndham. Can you catch him? Don't get caught. I send you an order about our fight at Kellysville. It was a hard fight and a glorious one for us, but the loss of the "gallant Pelham" has thrown a shadow of gloom over us not soon to pass away. Beckham will succeed him. Be vigilant about your own safety and do not have any established Hd. Qrs. anywhere but "in the saddle." I hope Mrs. Mosby reached you in safety. My regards to her if still with you. Your praise is on every lip, and the compliment the President has paid you is marked as it is deserved.

Very truly yours,
J.E.B. Stuart
Major General

Appreciation of Mosby from
The Photographic History
of the Civil War

From The Photographic History of the Civil War in Ten Volumes *(published 1911)*
Volume Four: The Cavalry
By Captain Charles Dudley Rhodes, member of the U.S. Army General Staff. Rhodes became a major general during World War I. He also wrote a book on the history of the cavalry of the Army of the Potomac.

Colonel John S. Mosby, with his raiding detachments of varying size, was probably the best known and the most anxiously sought by the Union forces of any of the partisan leaders. Mosby's absolute fearlessness, his ingenious methods of operating, as well as his innate love of danger and excitement, all combined to make his sudden descents upon the Federal lines of communication spectacular in the extreme.

His almost uniform success and the spirit of romance which surrounded his exploits drew thousands of recruits to his leadership, and had he desired, he could have commanded a hundred men for every one who accompanied him on his forays. But he continued throughout the war using small detachments of from twenty to eighty men, and much of his success was probably due to this fact, which permitted sudden appearances and disappearances. From beginning to end of the war, Mosby's raiders were a constant menace to the Union troops, and the most constant vigilance was necessary to meet successfully his skillfully planned stratagems.

On March 8, 1863, Mosby performed one of the most daring and effective feats of his career. In this case, as well as in others, it was the supreme boldness of the act which alone made it possible. Even with their knowledge of Mosby's methods, the Union officers could hardly conceive of such an apparently rash and unheard-of exploit being successful.

With a small band of carefully picked men, Mosby rode safely through the Union picket-lines, where the sentries believed the party to be Federal scouts returning from a raid. Upon reaching the vicinity of Fairfax Court House, Mosby entered the house used as headquarters by General Edwin H. Stoughton, woke the general, and demanded his surrender. Believing that the town had surrendered, the Union leader made no resistance. Meanwhile, each trooper in Mosby's little command had quietly secured several prisoners. Mosby and his cavalcade galloped safely back to their lines.

It was with similar strokes, original in conception and daring in execution, that Mosby kept thousands of Federal cavalry and infantry away from much-needed service at the front. After he became well established as a partisan ranger, his men were never organized as a tactical fighting body, and never had, as with other troops, an established camp. Through his trusty lieutenants, the call would be sent out for a designated number of men "for Mosby." This was the most definite information as to their mission that these volunteers ever received. In fact, they always moved out with sealed orders, but at the appointed time and place the rangers would assemble without fail. That Mosby wanted them was sufficient.

Many of these men were members of regular cavalry regiments home on furlough, others were farmers who had been duly enlisted in the rangers, and were always subject to call, still others were troopers whose mounts were worn out, and whose principal object was to secure Northern horses. The Union cavalry always claimed that among Mosby's men were a number who performed acts for which they were given short shrift when caught. Of course, the nature of the service performed by these rangers was subversive of discipline, and it is quite possible that many deeds were committed which the leader himself had absolutely nothing to do with and would not have sanctioned. But this is true with all warfare.

Mosby's expeditions often led him far within the Union lines and the command was often nearly surrounded. On such occasions Mosby would give the word and the detachment would suddenly disintegrate, each trooper making his way back to his own lines through forests and over mountains as best he could. But Mosby seemed to bear a charmed life, and in spite of rewards for his capture and all manner of plans to entrap him, he continued his operations as a valuable ally to the main Confederate army.

Mosby's Raiders, portrayed in the *Illustrated London News. Author's collection.*

Of course much of his success was due to the fact that he was ever operating in a friendly country. He could always be assured of authentic information, and wherever he went was certain of food, fresh horses, and means of concealment.

In 1864, Mosby was shot during one of his forays, and was left, apparently dying, by the Union troops, who failed to recognize him, in the house where he had been surprised. Learning soon after that the wounded Confederate was the famous leader of Mosby's rangers, the troops hastily returned to capture him or secure his dead body. But in the meantime, Mosby's men had spirited him away, and within a short time he and his men were again raiding Federal trains and outposts.

Until the end of the war he kept up his indefatigable border warfare, and it was not until after the surrender at Appomattox, that Mosby gathered his men about him for the last time, and telling them that the war was over, pronounced his command disbanded for all time.

Bibliography

PUBLICATIONS

Abramson, Rudy. *Hallowed Ground*. Charlottesville, VA: Thomason-Grant & Lickle, LLC, 1996.

Alexander, John Henry. *Mosby's Men*. New York: Neale Publishing Co., 1907.

Ashdown, Paul, and Caudill, Edward. *The Mosby Myth: A Confederate Hero in Life and Legend*. Wilmington, DE: SR Books, 2002.

Blumenson, Martin. *Patton: The Man Behind the Legend, 1885–1945*. New York: William Morrow, 1985.

Bonan, Gordon B. *The Edge of Mosby's Sword: The Life of Confederate Colonel William Henry Chapman*. Carbondale, IL: Southern Illinois University, 2009.

Brown, Peter A. *Mosby's Fighting Parson: The Life and Times of Sam Chapman*. Westminster, MD: Willow Bend Books, 2001.

Churchill, Winston. *The River War*. London: Longman, Green & Co., 1899.

Clifton, Irma C. *Fairfax County Stories: 1607–2007*. Springfield, VA: Goetz Printing Company, 2007.

Davis, William C., Brian C. Pohanka and Don Troiani. *Civil War Journal: The Leaders*. Nashville, TN: Rutledge Hill Press, 1997.

Evans, Thomas J., and James M. Moyer. *Mosby's Confederacy: A Guide to the Roads and Sites of Colonel John Singleton Mosby*. Shippensburg, PA: White Mane Publishing Co., 1991.

———. *Mosby Vignettes, Vol. I–V*. Privately published.

Flood, Charles Bracelen. *Lee: The Final Years*. Boston: Houghton Mifflin Company, 1981.

Gernand, Bradley E. *A Virginia Village Goes to War: Falls Church During the Civil War*. Virginia Beach, VA: The Donning Company Publishers, 2002.

Goetz, David. *Hell Is Being Republican in Virginia: The Post-War Relationship between John Singleton Mosby and Ulysses S. Grant*. Bloomington, IN: Xlibris Corp., 2012.

Grove, Noel, and Charles P. Poland. *The Lure of Loudoun*. Virginia Beach, VA: The Donning Company Publishers, 2007.

Guy, Anne Welsh. *John Mosby: Rebel Raider of the Civil War*. New York: Abelard-Schuman, 1965.

Hakenson, Donald C., and Gregg Dudding. *Mosby Vignettes, Vol. VI & VII*. Privately printed: Vol. VI, first printing, 2002; Vol. VII, first printing, 2003.

Jones, Virgil Carrington. *Ranger Mosby*. Chapel Hill: University of North Carolina Press, 1944, 1987.

Keen, Hugh C., and Horace Mewborn. *43rd Battalion Virginia Cavalry Mosby's Command*. Lynchburg, VA: H.E. Howard, Inc. 1993.

Melville, Herman. *Battle-Pieces and Aspects of the War*. New York: Harper and Brothers, 1866.

Mitchell, Adele H. *The Letters of John S. Mosby*. Richmond, VA: The Stuart-Mosby Historical Society, 1986.

Mosby, John S. *The Memoirs of Colonel John S. Mosby*. Nashville, TN: J.S. Sanders & Company, 1917, 1995.

Netherton, Nan and Ross, and Ruth Preston Rose. *In the Path of History*. Falls Church, VA: Higher Education Publications, Inc., 2004.

O'Neill, Robert F. *Chasing Jeb Stuart and John Mosby: The Union Cavalry in Northern Virginia from Second Manassas to Gettysburg*. Jefferson, NC: Frankland & Co., 2012.

Patton, Robert H. *The Pattons: The Personal History of an American Family*. New York: Crown Publishers, Inc., 1994.

Ramage, James A. *Gray Ghost: The Life of Col. John Singleton Mosby*. Lexington: University of Kentucky Press, 1999.

Robertson, James I, Jr. *Civil War Virginia*. Charlottesville: University Press of Virginia, 1991.

Scott, Major John. *Partisan Life with Colonel John S. Mosby*. Gaithersburg, MD: Old Soldiers Books, 1989.

Siepel, Kevin H. *Rebel: The Life and Times of John Singleton Mosby*. New York: St. Martin's Press, 1983, 2008.

Swanson, James L. *Manhunt*. New York: HarperCollins, 2007.

Ward, Geoffrey, and Ric and Ken Burns. *The Civil War: An Illustrated History*. New York: Alfred A. Knopf, Inc. 1990.

Wert, Jeffery D. *Mosby's Rangers*. New York: Simon and Schuster Paperbacks, 1991, 2011.

BROADCAST MEDIA

Get Lost in Loudoun: Hunting the Gray Ghost. http://www.youtube.com/watch?v=nbMo8ChzF8M.

The Gray Ghost (TV series, 1957–58). http://www.youtube.com/watch?v=UDL6Tzzm2oo&feature=related.

The History Channel: *Civil War Journal – The Gray Ghost: John Singleton Mosby* (1993). http://www.history.com/Civil+War+Journal+The+Gray+Ghost+John+Singleton+Mosby.

History of the Medical College of Virginia. www.medschool.vcu.edu/about/history/index.html.

Introduction to Colonel John Singleton Mosby: Fairfax County, Virginia. http://www.fxva.com/150/stories/mosby.

Mosby's Combat Operations in Fairfax County, Virginia. (A film by Don Hakenson, Charles V. Mauro and Steve Sherman, 2011). http://www.youtube.com/watch?v=8VzPsg6fLhs.

Mosby's Greenback Raid, October 1864 in Duffields, West Virginia, by Jim Surkamp. (http://www.youtube.com/watch?v=lxg1y4TpxXI&feature=related).

Mosby raider captured Colt 1860 Army Model percussion revolver. National Firearm Museum Treasure Gun. http://www.youtube.com/watch?v=sBXhGCQp1Cs&feature=related.

The Patriot (2000 film starring Mel Gibson). http://en.wikipedia.org/wiki/The_Patriot_%282000_film%29.

Index

About the Author

William S. Connery grew up in Baltimore, Maryland, considered to be "neutral territory" in the Civil War/War Between the States. As a young boy, his family visited the battlefields of Gettysburg, Antietam and Harpers Ferry and other local historical sites. He has a degree in history from the University of Maryland–College Park. He is married and has two sons. Since 1989, Mr. Connery has lived in Fairfax County, Virginia, where many thrilling and exciting skirmishes occurred. He has been contributing to the *Civil War Courier*, the *Washington Times* Civil War page and other publications. In 2012, he was awarded the prestigious Jefferson Davis Historical Gold Medal for his previous History Press book, *Civil War Northern Virginia 1861*. Mr. Connery is a member of the Company of Military Historians, the Capitol Hill Civil War Round Table, the Sloop of War Constellation Museum and the E.A. Poe Society of Baltimore. He is a frequently requested speaker on the Civil War and other American history topics in the Washington, D.C., metro region.

Visit us at
www.historypress.net
....
This title is also available as an e-book